The Descent of Alette

Also by Alice Notley

165 Meeting House Lane (1971)
Phoebe Light (1973)
Incidentals in the Day World (1973)
For Frank O'Hara's Birthday (1976)
Alice Ordered Me to Be Made (1976)
A Diamond Necklace (1977)
Songs for the Unborn Second Baby (1979)
Dr. Williams' Heiresses (1980)
When I Was Alive (1980)
How Spring Comes (1981)
Waltzing Matilda (1981)
Tell Me Again (1982)
Sorrento (1984)
Margaret & Dusty (1985)
Parts of a Wedding (1986)
At Night the States (1988)
From a Work in Progress (1988)
Homer's Art (1990)
To Say You (1993)
Selected Poems of Alice Notley (1993)
Close to Me and Closer . . . (The Language of Heaven) and *Désamère* (1995)

with Douglas Oliver
The Scarlet Cabinet (1992)

The Descent of Alette

Alice Notley

PENGUIN POETS

For Albert Edward Notley, Sr.

PENGUIN BOOKS
Published by the Penguin Group
Penguin Books USA Inc., 375 Hudson Street,
New York, New York 10014, U.S.A.
Penguin Books Ltd, 27 Wrights Lane,
London W8 5TZ, England
Penguin Books Australia Ltd, Ringwood,
Victoria, Australia
Penguin Books Canada Ltd, 10 Alcorn Avenue,
Toronto, Ontario, Canada M4V 3B2
Penguin Books (N.Z.) Ltd, 182–190 Wairau Road,
Auckland 10, New Zealand

Penguin Books Ltd, Registered Offices:
Harmondsworth, Middlesex, England

First published in Penguin Books 1996

17 19 20 18

Portions of this work first appeared in *Scarlet* magazine.
The Descent of Alette was published, in its entirety, in
The Scarlet Cabinet: A Compendium of Books by
Alice Notley and Douglas Oliver, Scarlet Editions, 1992.

Library of Congress Cataloging-in-Publication Data
Notley, Alice, 1945–
The descent of Alette / Alice Notley.
p. cm.
ISBN 0 14 05.8764 0 (pbk.)
I. Title.
PS3564.O79D47 1996
811'.54—dc20 95-32698

Printed in the United States of America
Set in Minion
Designed by Virginia Norey

Author's Note

A word about the quotation marks. People ask about them, in the beginning; in the process of giving themselves up to reading the poem, they become comfortable with them, without necessarily thinking precisely about why they're there. But they're there, mostly, to measure the poem. The phrases they enclose are poetic feet. If I had simply left white spaces between the phrases, the phrases would be rushed by the reader—read too fast for my musical intention. The quotation marks make the reader slow down and silently articulate—not slur over mentally—the phrases at the pace, and with the stresses, I intend. They also distance the narrative from myself, the author: I am not Alette. Finally they may remind the reader that each phrase is a thing said by a voice: this is not a thought, or a record of thought-process, this is a story, told.

Contents

Author's Note v

The Descent of Alette ix

BOOK one 1

BOOK two 43

BOOK three 83

BOOK four 119

About the Author 150

The Descent of Alette

BOOK
one

"One day, I awoke" "& found myself on" "a subway, endlessly"
"I didn't know" "how I'd arrived there or" "who I was" "exactly"
"But I knew the train" "knew riding it" "knew the look of"
"those about me" "I gradually became aware—" "though it seemed

as that happened" "that I'd always" "known it too--" "that there was"
"a tyrant" "a man in charge of" "the fact" "that we were"
"below the ground" "endlessly riding" "our trains, never surfacing"
"A man who" "would make you pay" "so much" "to leave the subway"

"that you don't" "ever ask" "how much it is" "It is, in effect,"
"all of you, & more" "Most of which you already" "pay to
live below" "But he would literally" "take your soul" "Which is
what you are" "below the ground" "Your soul" "your soul rides"

"this subway" "I saw" "on the subway a" "world of souls"

"On the subway" "we rode the trains" "Got on, got off" "Sat &
watched, sat" "& slept" "Walked from car to car" "Stood in stations"
"We were caught up" "in movement" "in ongoingness" "& in ongoingness"
"of voices," "for example" "Which of us spoke? did" "it matter?" "Who

saw what" "was being seen," "knew what" "was known?" "Gradually
what was seen" "became what I saw," "to me" "Despair & outrage"
"became mine too" "Sorrow" "became mine—" "To ride a" "mechanical"
"contrivance" "in the darkness" "To be steeped in" "the authority"

"of" "another's mind" "the tyrant's mind" "Life of bits & pieces"
"cars & scenes" "disconnected" "little dreams" "False continuum"
"mechanical time:" "What do we miss?" "What do we miss?" "Was there
once" "something else?" "There are animals" "in the subway" "But they"

"are mute & sad" "There are singers" "There are corpses" "There is
substance" "of darkness" "And emotion" "strong emotion" "The air"
"is all emotion"

"A woman entered" "a car I rode," "had a misshapen" "slowing foot; &"
"she wore" "thick-lensed glasses" ("her eyes were small," "over-focused")
"She carried a cup, announced," "'I need" "enough money—" "the amount
is eighteen dollars—" "to take my daughter above the ground" "for one
night" "just one night" "I promised her a night" "above the ground'"

"'Money will not" "be enough,'" "a woman said to her," "'Not just money,"
"he wants your things," "your small things," "your emblems," "all your
trappings" "You must give up" "to the tyrant" "all your flowers"
"all your carnations" "Or your cut hair" "Give him your hair"
"You must give him your jokes" "your best jokes," "he takes whatever—"

"Makes fun of it," "but uses it" "Give him your only" "silk scarf"
"your tiny" "turquoise pendant" "Your old-fashioned watch" "your copper
barrette" "& your nail polish" "Give him your lotion, your gardenia"
"perfume" "Give him your coat too" "But keep your sweater" "Let him take"
"what he wants" "from your wallet" "red leatherette coin purse" "& then

he'll let you" "go upstairs" "& walk around in" "our times" "He will smile"
"his boyish smile" "& let you go up there awhile'"

"There was a woman," "in a station," "with a guitar &"
"amplifier," "who sang" "sang a song" "that said this:"

"'As the old man lies dying" "in his bishop's robe & gown"
"surrounded" "by museum cases full of jewels" "& gold"
"shards of Venuses" "oldest potteries" "He" "is on exhibit"
"too" "as he is dying" "As we watch him," "the women,"

"we receive our" "emerald rings" "They grow"
"begin to grow" "around our fingers," "as we watch him"
"Because" "we're his loyal" "secretaries" "as we
watch him" "on exhibit" "always governing" "always ruling

as he lies dying" "He" "could die forever" "On exhibit"
"in his mansion" "in his Vatican" "in his Parthenon" "in his"
"admini-" "strative offices" "See" "in the emeralds"
("which can get murkier" "uglier") "an endless" "endless male

will" "But the tyrant" "is a mild man" "Look in our emeralds"
"& see shadows" "We are those" "against the green" "green
lush light" "We are weightless" "Left with rings,"
"we will be old &" "left with rings" "By the time the"

"lakes thaw the" "green lakes" "of the great cities"
"of the North" "We will be dead" "With emerald rings"
"Green stones upon our" "fingerbones" "That is our love"
"Must be our love" "that we" "will be dead &" "he"

"will live forever," "on exhibit" "in his museum'"

"I was standing up," "on the subway," "holding on to" "a metal
strap" "A man in" "an army jacket" "sat in front of" "me, eating"
"eating a piece of meat" "which he held" "in his hand," "a piece of
cold steak rimmed with fat" "& with black dots of pepper on it—"

"He gnawed the meat" "awhile, then" "looked up & said to me,"
"'I need to find" "our father" "our fathers . . .'" "'But what about"
"our mother?'" "I said auto-" "matically," "'the one mother"
"first mother" "of all?'" "He said nothing," "finished eating,"

"leaned back into" "his seat" "He was young," "familiar-looking
to me" "He fell asleep then" "his chin doubling" "as his head"
"fell forward" "He was brown-haired" ("brown-eyed, I'd seen")
"moustached &" "straight-nosed" "He spoke" "in his sleep—"

"'I need a dolor" "a few more dolors" "Then after that" "I'll see
our father'" "Another time" "he spoke & said," "'I'll give him
floral rocks" "floral rocks'" "After a while" "he awoke" "& said"
"to me, 'Shall we look for them?" "Or I'll" "look for him,"

"you" "look for her . . .'" "'Then yours" "would be easier" "much easier,'"
"I said with anger" "'But I am agonized,' he said" "'I killed for him,"
"I was a soldier'" "The train stopped" "He abruptly" "left the car"
"Disappeared" "disappeared"

"We couldn't find" "our fathers—" "there were several" "of us"
"We were walking through subway cars" "looking" "for our fathers" "Endless
train" "It seemed the longest" "train there is" "as if it circled"
"the world—" "& we walked it, we were searching" "for our fathers,"

"when we entered" "a car of" "suited . . . animals—" "men, actually,"
"in business suits," "clean shirts" "Charcoal suits, &" "navy-blue"
"ties (crimson stripes") "—beautiful suits—" "And the men all" "had
animal" "heads." "It was a dimly" "lit car" "the lights" "on occasion"

"would go completely:" "Darkness" "Silent" "Animal" "Faces" "Shaggy"
"or Sleek:" "He is a falcon, a gyrfalcon" "his head cocked toward his"
"business-suited" "wing-arm" "His eyes," "clear-dark-round," "stare"
"Or he's a lemur" "a reddish lemur" "reddish eyes" "fur, tipped in orange,

glows orange" "above his gray suit" "He's a panther, black sleek hair"
"You want to touch" "above his nose" "feel his short hair plush face,"
"black velvet" "He's an owl" "His face is feathers, it is ruffed,"
"his eyes are critical, a" "gray owl:" "Were these our fathers?" "And

if so, which" "was which," "who" "was my father" "your father?"
("And the men" "couldn't speak to us" "made no sound" "made no sign")
"Can you" "find your father?" "Mine is probably" "an owl" "He stared"
"He stared at me" "But owls stare" "And then he looked away"

" 'An animal-mother" "is crying,' " "a voice said" "to another (I"
"couldn't see them," "I was sitting—" "a crowded car:" "Bodies"
"pressed together" "Braid of voices" "& machine noise") " 'Animals
don't cry,' " "the second" "voice said" " 'She has large, furry forearms,'

the first continued," " 'Can you see her" "over there? She is showing"
"such sorrow' " " 'They don't do that,' the other said," " '& don't have"
"things like sorrow' " " 'You mean emotions?' said the first" " 'I
see her,' " "said the second," " 'Why" "is she wearing" "a dress? What"

"animal is she?' " " 'She is one,' " "said the first voice," " 'of the
large cats—" "a long-haired, large cat" "The species" "is thought to be"
"mostly" "extinct" "& for a long time—the gray-eyed" "brown-haired
"silky" "cat of the—" "I can't remember where, exactly—" "with a

musical—" "It's not a roar," "a softer sound" "It would blur" "into the
wind" "from high up on" "rocks & hills" "There were" "rocks & hills"
"where the cats lived" "where they once lived" "A dress was put on her"
"in the subway" "You can't ride this train" "without clothes" "Unless

you're crazy" "really crazy" "She has no one" "See her sorrow?' "
"The second" "voice replied," " 'They must be" "the only" "cats that cry,"
"what" "happened to them?' " "The first said, 'We don't know" "They
don't tell" "But we think" "her children—" "the children of" "her

generation—" "are suicidal," "eat datura," "have no real mates' "
" 'Animals,' " "said the second voice," " 'are not" "suicidal' " " 'I'll bet
she carries things,' " "the first said," " 'They carry things" "in their
pockets" "I'll bet she has" "a bit of snake bone" "a bit of creosote"

"a bit of tiny" "yellow blossom" "or other blossom" "A pebble"
"2 pebbles maybe" "A rusted bottlecap" "A piece of paper," "a scrap of it"
"A lock of fur" "clump of fur' " " 'I don't believe you,' said the
second voice," " 'She's an animal' "

"A mother" "& child" "were both on fire, continuously"
"The fire" "was contained in them" "sealed them off
from others" "But you could see the flame" "halo
of short flame all about the" "conjoined bodies, who

sat" "they sat apart" "on a seat for two" "at end of car" "The
ghost" "of the father" "sat in flames" "beside them"
"paler flames" "sat straight ahead" "looking
straight ahead, not" "moving." "A woman"

"another woman" "in a uniform" "from above the ground"
"entered" "the train" "She was fireproof" "She was gloves, & she"
"took" "the baby" "took the baby" "away from the"
"mother" "Extracted" "the burning baby" "from the fire" "they

made together" "But the baby" "still burned"
("But not yours" "It didn't happen" "to you")
"'We don't know yet" "if it will" "stop burning,'"
"said the uniformed" "woman" "The burning woman" "was crying"

"she made a form" "in her mind" "an imaginary" "form" "to
settle" "in her arms where" "the baby" "had been" "We saw
her fiery arms" "cradle air" "She cradled air" ("They take your
children" "away" "if you're on fire")

"In the air that" "she cradled" "it seemed to us there" "floated"
"a flower-like" "a red flower" "its petals" "curling flames"
"She cradled" "seemed to cradle" "the burning flower of" "herself gone"
"her life" ("She saw" "whatever she saw, but what we saw" "was that flower")

"A woman came into" "a car I rode" "about thirty-seven" "maybe
forty" "Face" "a harsh response to" "what she did" "had to do"
"face rigid" "but she was beautiful" "Was," "we could see,"
"one of the ones who" "strip for coins" "on the subway—"

"They simply" "very quickly" ("illegally") "remove all their
clothes" "Stand, for a moment" "Turning to face" "each end"
"of the car" "Then dress quickly," "pass quickly" "the cup."
"But she—this one—" "face of hating to so much that" "as she

took off her blouse," "her face" "began to change" "Grew
feathers, a small beak" "& by the time she was naked," "she wore the
head" "of an eagle" "a crowned eagle" "a raptor" "herself—"
"And as she stood" "& faced the car" "her body" "was changing"

"was becoming entirely" "that bird" "those wings," "she shrank to
become the bird" "but grew wings that" "were wider" "than she had been
tall" "Instantly," "instantly, a man caught her" "A cop came"
"As if ready" "as if they knew" "Her wings were clipped,"

"talons cut" "as if as quickly" "as possible" "She was released
then, to the car" "to the subway" "Perched" "on the bar the
straps hang from"

"I entered" "a car" "in which I seemed" "to see double"
"Each person I" "looked at seemed" "spread out" "as if doubled"
"Gradually" "I perceived that" "each person" "was surrounded by
a ghostly" "second image" "was encased in it" "& each"

"of those images," "those encasings," "was exactly the same"
"each was in fact" "the tyrant" "Though colorless," "a gray
ghost of him" "But he bent & swayed" "& walked with" "every
person, his" "expression" "always" "the same:" "mild &

benign" "And he encased many" "men not so" "uncomfortably"
"But others," "especially women," "looked as if they" "suffered from"
"trying" "to fit inside" "this other" "As if his form" "squeezed
theirs," "their breasts & hips," "very painfully—" "his long

thin streamlined form" "One woman" "tried to cast him off,"
"shake him off" "Writhed & jumped" "Then I felt him" "begin to
encase *me*" "He sank down" "into my head" "into my thoughts,"
"which instantly" "separated" "assumed a terrifying" "strict

order" "unfamiliar" "to me" "Each felt distinct" "from each,"
"arranged" "in a progression" "My head" "contained an
army" "of separate" "same-shape thoughts" "Soldiers"
"soldiers marching" "Never touching each" "other" "It wasn't"

"wasn't" "like a mind" "No thought felt true" "Thoughts felt
efficient" "He squeezed on me" "would squeeze away" "my shape"
"I cast him off" "& ran" "from the car"

"At a subway stop, crowds of people" "some sleeping" "on the
platform &" "Behind them," "caveish stores," "a row of stalls niched
in the walls" "A snake" "lives in this stop," "lies there" "on the
platform" "before a door—" "which is an exit—" "lies large

coiled & sleeping" "Women" "vaguely whorish" "come & go here,"
"they are ant-faced—" "smooth carnelian" "carapaces" "above bright-
colored" "cotton blouses" "There are men" "large-handed furry"
"They are round-eyed" "gray spiders" "But the snake sleeps" "before the

door that's" "an exit" "to the tyrant's world" "She is black,"
"gold, & brown" "Sleeps because" "she is sad" "is drugged by"
"melancholy" "Corpse-souls" "from the cemetery" "wander here" "near her
coils," "disturbed &" "white-dusty" "Too many of us" "underground"

"But we think" "the snake is growing" "She is growing; here's an
example:" "A woman" "who is standing," "waiting" "for the train,"
"is someone who" "will be allowed" "to exit—" "wears a business suit
big shoulders" "Her animal familiarity" "to us is" "powdered over,"

"pearlized" "She's attractive," "is suffused with" "her powers"
"a sense of" "her own powers" "But she" "is surrounded by" "a pale gel"
"a thick light" "a viscous" "transparency" "It sets her apart from us"
"Some other" "kind of will" "It is substance of" "the tyrant's thought"

"She belongs to" "the tyrant," "though she thinks she's" "her own"
"Now this is" "what happens:" "There is a figure" "in her body"
"another one, it" "steps out of it" "Leaves her body" "It is brown,"
"& naked" "Both humorous" "& shadowed" "of face—" "A spirit leaves her"

"& lies down by" "the snake" "Becomes ghostly" "brown coils"
"Disappears into" "the snake"

"A woman" "a crazed woman—" "seems crazy" "crouches naked,
in a corner"
"of the car" "Seems to try" "to stand up, it's as if her legs" "won't work"
"won't quite" "Or as if" "she can't remember" "if it's okay" "to be
naked," "if you're wearing a" "shawl" "an ugly shawl" "It's the color of"

"a dirty pale kitchen wall" "Now stands up" "She stands" "even though she is
naked" "Assumes a place here," "anyway" "How old is she?" "maybe, in her
fifties" "She is speaking" "Is it to us?" "Lips are moving," "speaks
softly," "but urgently:" "'No place no" "place" "except me" "No place"

"except under" "this shawl" "I can have" "*this place*" "I don't want you"
"Don't want it" "Please don't" "give me anything" "Money, clothes . . . ideas"
"What you think are" "yours'" ("Says to me,") "'It's all made by"
"a man" "You were made by" "men, made out of man-thought" "All
women now,

all of this here," "man-made—" "Under" "my shawl" "I try to be, I" "am"
"another world" "a woman's world—" "Why I may be" "the only one" "the
first one" "since before" "the tyrant's history" "So you must leave me
alone . . .'" "And then she left us" "unsteadily, walked away" "afraid of us"

"afraid" "we would corrupt her" "corrupt her world"

" 'When I was born," "I was born now" "fully grown," "on heroin" "When I
was born" "fully grown" "in the universe" "of no change" "nothing" "grows
up from' " ("Who sings this, whose voice?" "This person" "is in a shadow"
"down at the end of" "the platform" "I can't see him" "at all" "He continues

his song:") " 'When I was born," "I was now" "When I was born," "I'm not
allowed" "to remember when I was" "the little baby" "in a darkness, joy of
darkness" "Was I the cub" "for an instant?" "if so" "only an instant,"
"before I" "was a soldier" "before I" "was a soldier . . .' " ("Where is the

battlefield?" "At a station" "no longer" "in use" "Train goes right
past it" "But veterans" "know how" "to get in" "In that station" "is kept a
piece of" "a battlefield" "of the old war" "In that station" "grow white
flowers" "large blossoms" "that are faces," "with eyes closed" "lashes

closed white" "White skin white hair" "Soldiers go there" "Call to"
"the victim-flowers" "They don't answer but" "seem to grow" "The soldiers
water them" "water the flowers" "which were" "their own victims:")
" 'When I was born," "I was born now" "When I was born," "I'm not allowed"

"to remember if I was" "the little baby" "the little boy" "Was I the cub"
"for an instant?" "Or was I" "already" "a soldier . . .' "

"When the train" "goes under water" "the close tunnel" "is transparent"
"Murky water" "full of papery" "full of shapelessness" "Some fish" "but
also things" "Are they made by humans?" "Have no shape," "like rags"
"like soggy papers" "like frayed thrown-away wash cloths" "black"

"& encrusted with" "dirt & scum" "The fish" "move among them"
"& weeds which"
"grow black," "dirty in" "blackened water" "A fish, an" "immense fish"
"approaches" "our window" "A face as if" "to be recognized" "nuanced,"
"full of pain" "A face" "as of a man" "wide-eyed," "of course," "& gulping

but" "a face of" "a man" "No it's a fish face," "slime-encrusted" "Is
it a man" "or a fish?" "Someone stares," "stares back at him" "& cries"
"just a little" "She says, 'He's so sad-looking'" "His face changes"
"often changes" "as if we have him" "out of focus" "He blurs" "The

woman says," "'It makes me" "so uncomfortable," "that I can't"
"see him right'" "And the fish, too" "seems to weep" "moist blackish beads"
"He can't keep up" "with the window" "& is left behind" "Then the
woman says," "'He looked" "so familiar" "to me . . .'"

"There is a car" "that is nothing but" "garbage" "Shit &
spittle" "dropped food" "frayed brownness" "dirty matter"
"pressed down & flattened" "Paper piled" "piled on the floor"
"heaped on the benches" "Napkins yellowed" "tampons bloody"

"paper twisted" "torn & sodden" "Ashes &" "gray rags &"
"old skin & nails" "Old hair" "old bones" "& a Corpse"
"a skeleton corpse" "a skeleton in a" "dress, some sort of
old" "native dress" "of tattered skins" "animal skins"

"animal skins now brown-black," "coral beads now greasy" "She
lies against" "a mound of garbage" "at one end of" "the car"
"She has a small skull small finger bones" "a small woman"
"elegant skull" "The only ones" "who ride in this car" "are

those who" "take drugs" "So it's left this way—" "They"
"don't mind the smell" "They say" "she protects them"
"protects them from fearfulness," "by being" "the gentle fearful"
"herself" "They don't" "touch her though" "They say she hums"

"like a motor" "Or something does" "in the garbage"
"Something" "is still alive in there," "has power"

"I walked" "into a car" "No one there" "There was no one" "But
there were voices" "I heard voices" "All of these voices"
"were like beggars" "beggars' voices" "the voices crowded" "together"
"intoning" "like beggars:" "'Spare? Spare any?" "Spare any mothers?"
"fathers?" "Spare any, I won't" "hurt you," "lady," "My body" "Spare a
new" "new body?" "body?" "Today" "is my old" "baby's birth-

day, do you have" "any change?" "My old baby" "is gone but" "Change"
"Spare any" "Old babies" "Young fathers" "Spare any" "generations" "of
mine, Can you" "spare" "my mother" "a mother" "Spare any . . . ?'"
"And on louder" "& the phrases" "more crowded" "together" "The car
seemed
empty" "but I" "was afraid" "to sit down" "Gradually," "as I stood there,
still afraid" "to move" "too afraid of" "bumping into" "an invisible"

"person," "somehow I" "began to see" "the voices," "or their
locations" "A window" "black window, both" "rigid, &" "rushing"
"A gray bench place, dirty" ("the usual, sharpened" "by sound") "A
space" "in the middle of" "the car" "through which you looked" "at a
picture" "of a tropical" "island" "& words:" "*Fly to Heaven*"
"'Spare," "spare" "a spare heaven" "spare a city'" "'Look at me,'

said a voice," "'I am dying.'" "I looked" "at his voice &" "saw another"
"silver pole" "'I'm dying,'" "he said" "fiercely" "rather proudly"
"'Look at me I'm dying'" "I couldn't see him, I still" "couldn't see him"
"'Look at me I'm dying" "Give me change" "Give me change'" "I
couldn't see him"

"In one car people work" "seem to work there" "It's their office"
"But when you enter it you" "see them" "perform actions" "without objects"
"As if in pantomime" "Without papers" "without machines" "Most of
these are women" "They wear dresses," "pantyhose," "grown-up shoes,"

"& makeup" "They carry" "leather pocketbooks" "And they do things"
"continuously" "with their hands" "Perform motions" "of working"
"Work invisible" "keyboards" "carry invisible" "files," "invisible
papers" "Hold up airy" "phone receivers" "against hairdos"

"& move their lips" "say silent words" "They are working, working"
"Then a man" "in a suit" "enters" "& they hand him" "all their
invisible work" "He goes through it" "as if page by page" "& scrutinizes
air" "with a grave," "lined face" "Sometimes smiles with" "mild

approval" "Appears to think" "hard" "Goes quiet" "They watch him as"
"he picks up" "the invisible" "phone receiver" "His lips" "begin to
move" "He motions" "the women" "to resume their work"

"At a station" "there's a mirror" "a black mirror" "Just a mirror"
"on the platform" "where the train stops" "But it's solid black"
"When you look in it, you" "see a mask" "your mask" "It's your
present mask," "I guess" "I looked in it" "& saw" " . . . a benign

plain wooden mask" "plain mask" "nothing special" "just a brown mask"
"Another woman" "standing near me" "looked" "& saw a mask with a"
"snakelike face" "fangs" "& thin tongue" "golden eyes" "flat head (eyes had
cut-out" "dead pupils" "of a mask)" " 'I had a dream,' she said" "last

night" "I was angry," "& then" "was a snake" "Armless, legs together, into
one, I" "drew myself up" "snakelike" "to my full height—" "all length
& head—" "& lunged at" "a tall man," "like the tyrant," "who was im-
passive" "who watched me," "watched my anger," "as if I were" "a

small child" "I don't know why" "I was so angry" "in the dream" "What
had happened, but" "my striking" "out at him" "had no effect" "He only
looked at me" "kept looking," "calmly" "I had become" "unreason"
"And I had become" "despair" "He was reason" "I was despair,"

"it was as if with" "my moment" "of anger" "with him I had" "ruined my
life" "had shown myself" "estranged from" "the world" "I was
anger" "I was other" "I was now nothing but" "lost" "He didn't care"
"I was nothing" "nothing" "to him, & I" "continued to" "strike at him"

"unsuccessfully' "

" 'I once" "found an exit" "from the subway' " ("the woman told me")
" 'I once" "found a staircase" "that led to" "an exit" "temporarily
unlocked" "I opened the door to—" "It was an" "Antarctic"
"light, up there" "As if dawn or dusk, but" "neither" "Everyone

wore black" "black cashmere" "discreet diamonds" "had guarded,
dark eyes" "Was it" "the winter holidays?" "I saw" "crushed-red lights"
"reflected" "in snowy puddles" "White lights" "in naked trees"
"For me it" "was frozen time," "from past pain," "from a time"

"when I was young," "before I came beneath," "came down here—" "before
I'd willingly" "walked away from" "that upper world," "had left"
"a university—" "I then remembered from" "long before" ("as I stood"
"near the exit") "a library I'd entered" "in that partial light, in

Spring" "There was grass," "there were blossoms" "Huge windows"
"looking out on grass" "And shelves" "of books" "all the books there
were:" "The books were decayed matter," "black & moldy" "Came apart"
"in my hands" "All the books were" "black rot" "Were like mummies"

"More body of" "the tyrant" "It is all his body" "The world is" "his
mummy" "Up there, up there" "Down here it is" "a more desperate"
"decay," "as if" "rich emotion," "pain," "could still transform us"
"despite him" "despite his power, &" "tyrannical" " . . . ignorance,"

"passing as" "knowledge—" "And so of course I" "re-entered" "re-
entered" "the subway—" "I can't leave it" "ever" "unless"
"we all leave—' "

" 'Once,' she continued," "'years ago, the tyrant" "was shot"
"We saw it happen" "onscreen" "He was shot by" "a masked
assassin" "at close range—" "Blood spurted" "from his chest & head"
"A mother," "someone's mother" "came & cradled" "his head in

her lap" "There was wind & rain," "wind &
black rain" "His flesh colorless," "he seemed dead"
"Blood—" "his blood—" "was smeared onto" "the camera lens—"
"He didn't die." "A few weeks later, he" "reappeared onscreen"

"Announced he'd been" "in a coma," "then had recovered" "His
white hair was" "strangely reddish" "He said he'd been" "near death"
"He said he'd seen" "a white light" "forgiving" "all-embracing"
"He said he'd shed" "his blood for us" "But it was worth it" "worth it"

"for that," "that light" "which would, he now knew," "embrace us all"
"Which does" "include all" "That's when I knew,' she said," "'light
meant lie" "That's when I knew that" "the Light" "was a lie,"
"& that" "I would never" "seek light" "I will never" "seek light,' "

"she repeated" "before she boarded" "her train"

"A while before" "I entered" "the subway," "all money
underground" "became diseased" "It seared your skin," "when you
touched it" "& poisoned" "your bloodstream" "Within days,"
"you would die" "Thus all money" "was taken" "by people in"

"special suits &" "burned" "No more was issued" "here below—"
"So money" "became invisible" "Invisible money" "began to
change hands" "Paid" "in invisible" "Things paid for"
"by invisible . . ." "Everyone knows," "everyone knows"

"if you have it or not" "if you have enough or not" "All is
exactly as" "before" "when there was money," "except"
"it isn't printed" "isn't seen" "But it is money"
"just the same" "Thus," "there was a woman" "who kept trying"

"to leave the subway" "She was pointed" "out to me" "at a
station," "in process of" "trying to leave us" "A young woman,"
"curly-headed" "with a slightly" "loony look," "encased"
"in a large" "plastic container" ("people wear them" "when they

leave here") "She passed through" "the turnstile" "The other
side of" "the turnstile" "being obscured to us, as if" "everything on
that side" "were somehow" "blurred for us," "were viewed by us
myopically—" "I couldn't see" "exactly" "what happened:"

"movement of figures," "then" "she was" "returned to us,"
"sent back through in" "the plastic" "'They *never*" "let me leave"
"I get my plastic," "I get my money" "but they always" "turn me
back" "There's always" "something wrong with" "my money" "Usually

they say," "it's not enough" ("though" "it always is") "This time they
said it was" "too old" "I must have saved it too long" "Old money"
"isn't used" "anymore" "above the ground'" "'Why do you want"
"so much to go there?' I asked" "'Anyone does,'" "she said fiercely"

"I surprised myself" "by saying" "with conviction," "'*I don't*'"

"A man" "in a suit" "in the first car the" "front car of the train—"
"This older" "distinguished man" "asked me to" "ride with him"
"join him" "I declined &" "moved back" "far back, I" "joined a
car" "that contained" "women &" "girl children" "women in skirts"

"girls in dresses" "I wondered" "who the man was, why he wasn't"
"above the ground" "He must work for" "the tyrant" "But I forgot him
among our flags—" "we had a multitude" "of flags" "Some were red"
"red & wildly torn" "Some were silken" "almost flimsy" "Some were

spangled" "Some were lacy" "One girl carried one" "with a snake"
"appliquéd on it" "And one woman had" "the largest flag" "It said—"
"in gold letters" "that were burning," "in gold that showed through
flame" "which followed" "the letters' shapes—" "on white unburning

silk—" "said *Presence*" "*Presence*" "But the burning" "letters
shifted" "when the man entered" "our car" "the distinguished man in a
suit" "He sat down" "Did he only" "want to look at us?" "For he was
sitting" "there, staring" "And the letters" "the burning letters"

"shifted" "& changed" "to spell *Poverty*" "instead of *Presence*"
"He didn't need" "to ride the train" "He'd made us poor" "in an instant"
"They walk by" "& make you poor" "They look at you & make you poor"
"Surreptitiously I began" "to remove my" "bits of jewelry" "my earrings"

"with small citrines" "my ring of" "mismatched garnets" "I put them"
"in my pocket" "They weren't" "good enough"

"In a station" "I saw" "a woman crying" "She stood against"
"the wall" "looking dirty" "& exhausted," "crying quietly"
"I asked her who she was" "& why" "she was crying" "She
said: 'I" "am a painter" "I have been trying" "to find"

"a form the tyrant" "doesn't own—" "something" "he doesn't
know about" "hasn't invented, hasn't" "mastered" "hasn't
made his own" "in his mind" "Not rectangular," "not a
sculpture" "Not a thing at all—" "he owns all things,"

"doesn't he?" "He's invented" "all the shapes" "I'm afraid he's"
"invented mine," "my very own" "body'" ("she was hysterical")
"'Did he invent me?" "I want" "to do something like
paint air" "Perhaps" "I even want to" "invent air" "I've

painted" "thin transparent" "pieces" "of plastic" "They—"
"the pictures on them—" "always turn" "rectangular," "circular"
"I once painted" "on bat's wings" "I caught a bat" "painted
colors on" "let it loose &" "watched the air change . . ."

"He owns form," "doesn't he?" "The tyrant" "owns form'"

"A beautiful" "gaunt woman, a" "birdlike" "dark woman"
"Large tall, erect" "in a white dress a" "long robe"
"Head in profile, cowled head" "& she cradles" "a baby"
"dead baby" "Its spirit," "which seems a grown man," "rises"

"into black" "We are at" "a large, black-ceilinged"
"station" "Has a baby" "or a man died?" "She cradles"
"a dead baby" "But a man has died, he is rising" "into the air"
"It isn't" "isn't night sky up there, it's a black" "black

ceiling" "He will not" "continue" "to rise to" "the sky"
"We are confined below" "confined" "He sinks again" "Stands
on the floor" "while his mother, unseeing" "still cradles"
"the baby" "he once was" "They are near a decaying wall"

"crumbling, full of holes" "Another landscape" "shows beyond it"
"Seems to light up" "to appear to us" "A large, unbounded
space" "full of a throng of" "the Recent Dead" "Spirits,
all spirits" "A forest a city" "of white" "transparent

shimmering" "spirits" "close together" "And one" "one
disengages" "Comes toward the man" "Raises thin arms, has an
open" "dark mouth hole, says," "'Welcome" "to you dead man"
"we cannot rise, as we should" "We cannot pass through"

"the tyrant's world's" "new fabrics" "the materials
of his world" "He has changed" "the chemical" "composition"
"of everything" "but spirit" "but our souls" "but us—"
"We" "who are nature" "when nothing else is," "we are all

trapped below" "We can only go" "down" "farther down—"
"Down" "is now the only way" "to rise" "Come & wait with us"
"wait with us" "to descend'"

"A car" "awash with blood" "Blood at our feet" "& I
& others" "have small springs" "of blood from our"
"feet & knees" "There is an inch or two" "of blood"
"all over" "the car floor" "Replenished" "Periodically"

"by our body springs" "of blood" "And trickling out"
"the door," "when it opens" "at stations." "The
tyrant" "sends a hologram" "a life-sized hologram" "of
himself" "into our car" "He stands mid-car" "& says:"

" 'The blood at our" "feet" "has cost me" "so much"
"The blood" "at our feet" "has cost us so" "much"
"To clean" "the blood" "is difficult" "to clean the
car.' " "There is a litter" "of things" "in the

wash of blood" "I see sanitary" "pads," "kleenex,"
"black-blood encrusted" "old bandages" "An old black
suitcase" "spills out" "torn men's clothes" "& frayed towels"
"The hologram tyrant" "says, 'Here" "are my tears' " "Holds

up his palm" "His tears are" "small drops of jade"
"Red" "& white jade" "His tears have turned to jade"
"They will be placed in" "a National" "Museum" "There is
something in" "my ear" "I pull it out a" "white cord"

"a long" "silk cord" "I pull it out &" "hear our blood"
"It hums" "a unison one" "note loud a" "sheet of sound"
"It hangs there" "sad insect noise" "insect-like"
"Our blood."

"Two people fucking" "behind the stairs" "that led" "to other
trains" "The woman & man," "fucking," "had grown wings" "gray
feathered," "Subway gray, and" "the wings" "would beat the air"
"or stir the air, slightly" "Pause" "then encircle" "the back of"

"the other lover," "as arms" "gray wing arms" "The two lovers"
"were not naked" "They had feathers" "they had grayness" "Though they
had" "pink genitals" "in the midst of" "gray feathers, and"
"heads" "of dark hair" "Had dark hair," "dark

heads touching" "There's no place to" "make love"
"down here" "in the subway" "except near others"
"near all the others" "Like animals" "elegant animals"
"As in the days" "when there were animals" "animals in

the world" "Before the tyrant" "became everything" "before the tyrant"

"I saw" "a black flower" "growing" "from the platform"
"It was" "a small flower" "petunia-like" "black,"
"growing up from" "gray cement" "dirty" "bespattered non-earth"
"Small black" "like black blood" "like crushed-velvet black blood"

"As I looked at it" "it seemed" "to enlarge" "As I came nearer,"
"as if" "by my attention" "it enlarged more" "& I entered it,"
"I was it, for a time" "was that black blood crushed velvet" "velvet
womb, I guessed" "womb of Hell" "I was womb" ("was I

also dead?") "& inside it" "inside me" "in the center"
"was a seed that was" "an eye" "a small eye" "a blue eye"
"pale blue" "And smaller," "its black pupil" "Look"
"inside the pupil" "Inside the pupil's the" "black flower," "again"

"enormous" "crushed velvet" "black blood" "But
whose eye" "whose" "would it be?" "If it was mine," "whose
was that," "who" "would I be?" "Did it matter" "to me?" "Since really I"
"was womb?" "blood-black." "And would always" "again"

"become that"

"I walked" "into a car where" "everything was membrane-
like" "thin-membrane petal-like" "& veined"
"Fetus-like" "fetus-flesh-like" "In shades of pink" "purple black &"
"brown" "Thin" "reddish veins" "Fetal flower" "soaked in

subway light" "The car walls were translucent" "orchid-
flesh" "The seats were & the floor—" "All was naked flesh"
"We were naked" "A fetus" "delicate" "tiny-faced," "eyes closed,
concentrating" "curled" "almost spiraling," "floated high" "in the

air." "We sat naked on our" "membrane-like" "tan benches"
"All of us" "smooth & wrinkled" "brownish, or"
"darker," "or paler," "palest" "were as if" "within a flower"
"as if" "within us" "This" "This is" "simultaneous," "I understood"

"Uncontrolled by" "the tyrant" "Someone else"
"in all of us" "is this lovely" "fetal flesh," "flower skin"
"We are being this" "this flower" "And then" "the flower
vanished" "I was clothed, there was" "no fetus" "Gray subway car

of people" "riding quietly some sleeping" "Someone's earphones"
"turned up too loud" "buzzing wire" "vaguely song"

"Eyeball" "single eye" "a lashed eye" "funny eye"
"looking all around" "from the floor of a" "subway car"
"It's self-propelled" "moves in scurries" "near my foot"
"What's it looking for?" "It's so funny" "Its eye-

lashes" "are black" "demarcated" "They have wit, it has"
"wit" "This eyeball's funny" "on the gray floor"
"among round stains" "& ashes" "Looks all over"
"the car" "Expressive" "only looking, but" "stretching, in a"

"struggle" "to see" "Rolls about in" "itself," "& looks"
"I guess it's blue-eyed" "dark-blue" "No eyebrows, of
course" "Doesn't blink much" "Intent" "intent on looking"
"What's it looking for?" "I guess, whatever"

"In a large" "subway station" "a non-descript man tells us,"
" 'We'd like you" "to meet the tyrant—" "The real tyrant is not"
"the tall man in a dark suit" "That man is" "his representative"
"this man" "is the real" "tyrant . . .' " "He presents to us" "a large

man, pale—" "oh yes he's ghoulish" "As if he's what we'd" "expect,"
"really" "expect" "He smiles sheepishly at us" "He has a large face,"
"longish white hair" "Dark" "blue eyes" "all iris no white,"
"like cracked" "sapphires" "like jewel inserts" "in skull sockets"

"And his jaw" "is decaying" "pulpy soft" "oozy jaw" "His jaw"
"is decomposing" "That must be right for" "a figure" "of evil?"
"They want us" "to hate *him*," "if the tyrant" "must be hated"
"I say," " 'He's a substitute" "He's not the tyrant" "He's a simple

ghoul" "The tyrant" "is a mild-" "looking man" "He does not show"
"his decay" "He has no such grace," "you might say" "His sense of"
"his own knowledge" "presumed rightness" "preserves him" "forever"
"He could have never" "have never" "been that wrong:" "That thousands"

"upon thousands" "of years" "of enslavements" "so many different kinds"
"be integral to" "the solid" "& beautiful" "structures" "cathedrals"
"museums" "& mansions" "& temples" "he has built" "above the ground?"
"How could that be?' " "The non-descript man" "missed my irony" "& led"

"the ghoul away" "to meet another" "small group in" "the subway"

"I was standing" "in a room" "in a station—" "Had found a
place like" "a room," "an abandoned" "shop, perhaps" "I was en-
closed," "a private space" "The room was dark" "with a pale
whitish light" "resembling moonlight" "that shone in through"

"a burnt-out" "glassless window" "A man I knew"
"had joined me" "We stood talking" "in dark rubble," "I"
"near the window," "when the man" "assumed a look of"
"calm alarm" "on his face" "& pointed to" "something" "be-

hind me" "I turned & saw a" "head" "upsidedown" "in the
window" "An old man's face" "vaguely" "familiar—"
"old," "& white-haired," "looking friendly" "upside down"
"drooling" "just a little—" "old man who" "can't help that"

"I wanted" "to show" "my companion" "that I wasn't"
"afraid of" "this old man," "this familiar" "sudden old man, so I
patted" "his cheek" "his upside-down" "cheek" "He smiled,"
"& disappeared" "I gasped & said," "'That was the?'" "'tyrant,'"

"the man finished" "He looked annoyed" "'You hypocrite" "Or is it
sucker?'" "'Both,' I said" "'But in one way" "he is just" "an
old man'" "The man said," "'You've just patted" "the cheek of"
"the man" "you must confront" "& vanquish'"

"A car" "I was in" "became filled with" "an owl"
"A huge owl" "huge wings spread out" "huge owl face" "The owl was"
"a great" "horned owl" "a strange color" "of blue"
"a midnight blue" "as if an owl who" "was a night sky somehow,"

"a piece of night sky" "The owl's eyes" "were intent, intense"
"the beak dangerous" "But I was" "entranced" "'How
are you here?' I asked him" "He said, 'I am" "a projection"
"from another place" "am not so large" "Am a simple" "owl"

"I've come here" "to say" "that when you finally" "meet with
the tyrant—" "do you know yet" "you must confront him?'"
"I said nothing" "'Well, anyway,' he continued," "'when you
meet him," "I will help you" "I will help you, that is,"

"if you don't" "hurt anyone—" "anyone except" "the tyrant'"
"'What must I do to him?' I asked" "'What" "the situation" "will
require,' he said," "'but I think he" "must die'" "'Die?"
"I can't kill someone" "I can't kill," "I have no right'" "'You

are an animal,' said the owl," "'an animal" "as I am" "Act like
an animal" "when you kill him" "As little" "as possible"
"must happen" "It must be clean'" "'I have no prowess,' I said"
"'I will help you" "as I said'" "Then he left," "disappeared"

"I thought, 'That" "was my father," "I think" "that that owl"
"is probably" "my dead father'"

"I changed cars, on a train" "I felt distraught" "& had to move around"
"There was something" "trying," "in my head, to" "swim up," "a bad
dream" "Then I screamed—" "it was leaving" "my head" "I screamed"
"before everyone" "in the car" "It had burst out of me," "& we could

see it" "It was a dreamed man" "a man I'd never" "seen before"
"He was young I guess" "handsome" "dark-haired brown eyes" "He
had a knife" "& he killed himself" "before us" "With a knife he"
"stabbed his own neck" "deeply" "There was a jet of blood dark" "purple"

"across the car" "There was blood on me" "He vanished" "But there was
blood" "real blood" "on my leg & on no one else" "Though some had stood"
"just as close" "Everyone" "came to comfort me" "A youngish" "brown-
skinned woman" "in a cotton flower print" "took a handkerchief from her

purse" "& wiped the blood off" "my leg" "'It's as if *I* killed him,'"
"I said" "Will I always" "feel guilty?'" "'It's not your fault,' someone
said" "Then voices" "surrounded me" "with comfort" "caressing shadows:"
"*'You didn't do it'*" "'As if," "I said," "'I didn't love him" "enough'"

"They were somber" "for a moment" "Then one man said—" "in jeans" "& a
handkerchief" "tied round his head," "brown-skinned—" "said, 'The key"
"isn't always" "the word 'love'" "The key is literal" "A key'" "He held
a key in" "his hand" "then put it back into" "his pocket" "Literal

key" "literal blood" "'What is" "literal love?'" "I asked him" "'It is
this,'" "he said" "He took a pen knife" "from his pocket" "a small knife
but sharp" "'Hold very still'" "He made a cut on—" "'Hold still'" "He
cut my chest," "above the breast" "a small incision &" "it bled" "down my

blouse" "'Only your own blood" "is on you now" "is on you now,'"
"he said" "'It washes" "his away'"

"I stood again" "on the platform" "of the station" "where the snake
sleeps" "Stood near" "the snake herself," "in the shadows there,"
"thinking" "I felt poised" "to be decisive" "be decisive in some way"
"But only knew" "the same decision:" "Get on the next train" "or not"

"The snake" "the sad snake" "opened bleary dark" "gold-ringed eyes—"
"crusty sticky" "around their edges" "Opened eyes" "& opened mouth"
("I'd never seen her" "awake") "Extended" "a black tongue" "& said in"
"a woman's whisper:" " 'When I was" "the train," "when I was" "the train,"

"flesh & blood" "flesh & blood" "took you to your" "destination"
"to your life" "to your life" "carried you through your life" "Flesh &
blood were" "your life" "Flesh & blood were" "your time" "A soul"
"was not so naked," "so pained &" "denied" "abused &" "denied,"

"when I was" "the train . . .' " " 'You're not big enough,' " "I said to her,"
" 'not big enough to" "be a train' " "She ignored me" "& repeated" "over"
"& over," " 'When I was" "the train" "When I was" "the train" "When
I was" "the train . . .' " "until she" "finally" "fell asleep again"

"On a train, I" "fell asleep" "& dreamed I turned away" "from light:"
"I was reading" "I was reading" "an old book brown leather" "I
walked" "as I read" "I was reading" "& walking" "On a grassy"
"path that led" "to a small house" "up to its door" "I opened

the door—" "The house was filled with" "filled with white light"
"The tyrant stood there" "white-haired, round-blue-eyed" "black-suited,"
"& slim," "light" "all about him" "I turned & ran." "I awoke then"
"& thought," "'He owns enlightenment" "all enlightenment" "that we

know about" "He owns" "the light" "I must resist it'" "I slept again"
"My head" "fell against" "someone's shoulder, I" "jerked awake,"
"peered at a car of" "quiet men," "sleeper's mask each" "the smooth
eyelids," "the subtle modeling" "near each line of mouth" "I slept"

"& dreamed again:" "The tyrant floated" "in a blue sky" "He had
frayed edges" "all about himself," "became tatter-like" "His hair &
face," "his suit & hands" "were like rags blown" "on a clothesline"
"his eyes" "were bulging," "his mouth open" "His tatter-arms

stretched out" "his white thin hair blowing" "He became" "pieces of
cloth; sky" "appeared" "between the pieces" "which scattered" "He
blew away" "Where he had been was" "a chaos" "cavelike," "cave-
shaped a" "blue-black" "cell of winds" "The cave stretched backwards"

"into the blue sky a" "black" "snakelike tunnel"

"I was in a car" "with huge holes" "in the floor," "& in the
walls" "Each time I" "looked at them" "they seemed larger"
"There was hardly" "any floor to" "stand on" "I pressed myself"
"against a pole" "At my feet" "through the floor" "the tracks

gleamed," "slid by in darkness" "& the walls" "let in darkness"
"through spaces" "shaped like missing slats" "There was less & less"
"car there" "It became" "its own skeleton" "When the train"
"finally stopped I" "inched my way" "around the edges" "of where the

floor had been" "& out the door" "The station" "had a sign"
"hung above it" "which said" "*Tyrant's Head*" "It was dimly lit,"
"almost dark" "Strange clouds hung" "in front of it" "like eyes,
nose, & mouth:" "I walked through them" "into the semi-dark" "There was

a dress dummy to my right" "dressed up queenlike" "in a long dress,"
"jewels," "sash & crown" ("ragged hemline," "diamonds sooty")
"There were masks" "on the wall" "made out of garbage:" "old news-
papers & rags" "& gray" "cotton wadding" "There was a button" "on a

pedestal" "to be pressed &" "when I pressed it," "lights went on"
"The queen's jaw moved" "She smiled & said, 'Our" "stripper"
"will now give a" "command performance'" "The lights dimmed again"
"into a spotlight" "on a woman" "in a black dress" "a long dress"

"She began" "to undress:" "everything she wore" "was black"
"When she dropped her skirt, she said," "'This is my love'" "When she
unbuttoned" "her blouse &" "slid it off she" "said, 'This is my vision'"
"When she removed" "her bra" "she said," "'This is my life'" "She

stood before me" "in a black" "thong G-string" "& high heels"
"She slid" "the G-string off" "'No one is sure,'" "she said," "'if this
is positive or negative," "it just is'" "She slid the G-string on & off"
"repeatedly" "& repeated" "what she'd said," "'No one is sure" "if this is

positive or negative," "it just is'" "Finally" "the queen said,"
"'Thank you, that's enough'" "'I must" "finish stripping,'" "said the
stripper" "She began" "to masturbate with" "her finger" "saying
over" "& over," "'Invent the world" "Invent the world" "so I can

come again'" "After" "she had come—" "in a seconds-long" "weak spasm—"
"she turned into" "the tyrant" "The queen" "took his arm" "They both
bowed &" "the station" "became pitch-dark"

"There is a car in" "two worlds," "both worlds, the upper" "&
lower" "It is here" "in the lower" "every" "other second &"
"in the upper" "every other," "thus flickers as if" "strobe-light-
lit" "I can't enter it" "I can only" "look in" "at a window" "be-
tween the cars:" "I had been told to" "go look at"

"the man" "who wants to change things" "He is a large man in
fatigues," "vaguely round-faced" "& dark-haired—" "flickering—"
"Others—" "a few are women—" "similarly dressed," "flash"
"between the two worlds" "Hard to focus" "So hard to see them" "They
have various" "guns," "cartridge belts" "Converse" ("though I can't

hear them" "Such a roar in" "my ears" "between the cars")
"The man who" "wants to change things" "has a creature" "a small
creature" "on his shoulder" "At first I think it's a" "monkey"
"but gradually (they flicker so)" "I perceive that it's a"
"woman" "a tiny woman" "naked, & brown, with a" "chain" "that extends"

"from her neck—" "a small collar—to" "his belt" "He strokes her
head" "as he speaks" "Something" "is making him" "sad" "He
weeps" "His tears are hard, like" "the tyrant's," "small jewels"
"blue crystals" "A man picks them up" "from the floor" "& collects
them in a" "leather pouch" "The woman," "tiny woman," "has

aboriginal" "features, a" "wide nose a wide mouth" "eyes are wide
apart" "wiry hair" "face of knowing" "face of humor—" "sad
humor now—" "shiny-souled, she" "is perfect" "But her eyes" "I
gradually realize" "are gray" "look like mine" "look" "just like
mine" "And on the walls there are posters" "of men" "hero-leaders,"

"I guess, of" "rebel armies," "revolutions" "flickering, vibrating"
"& there floating," "flickering" "in space as if" "detaching, are"
"two eyes" "two gray spots" "two eyes that look like mine"

" 'What have we" "to do" "with the tyrant?' " "said a woman" " 'He somehow keeps us here" "but in my life I" "must have my life,"
"must squeeze my life out of" "being here" "Must be here" "since I
am' " "She was crying" "A dark woman" "large-

faced" "comfortably fleshed-out" "Her eyes" "shut the tears in"
"then opened" "again," " 'A life gets closer to" "being over" "You've
only done what" "he makes you do—" "because he says" "what a life is"
"And yet something else goes on" "For example" "when I curve" "my arms"

"just so," "I am a grotto" "of diamonds' " "I looked & saw that" "she was"
"was a curved" "rock wall" "studded" "with black" "faceted jewels"
"She curved towards me" "a dark shining" "I wanted" "to stand enclosed by" "As if you could" "stand upright en-" "veloped" "by a

geode—" " 'But no one knows," "no one sees,' " "I said"
" 'His great failure—" "the tyrant's failure—" "& yours too?' she
said," " 'is to think that" "achievement" "must be evident,"
"in the light—' " "The black gems spoke now" "There were purple-black"

"amethysts" "among them" "small purple lights—" " 'What you make"
"is nothing" "unless it's dark" "Darker than this" "And in the dark"
"in the great dark' " " 'What do you mean?' " " 'In the dark" "Made
in the dark" "Reflecting darkness" "Only darkness' "

"As I stood" "in a station" "looking into" "the tunnel,"
"I saw" "disembodied" "lights" "coming toward us" "Then I realized"
"a black train" "a solid black train" "was arriving" "at the station"
"It stopped" "The doors opened" "I entered, & sat down" "& then"

"a voice announced:" "'This particular" "train" "will leave the subway"
"for another," "deeper," "unilluminated place," "where all is"
"uncharted" "If you want" "to travel with us," "listen first:"
"The sides" "of the train," "the train's form will" "fall away"

"All will" "become a darkness" "in which each of you" "will also
lose form" "We can't say" "what happens then" "We don't know how
you'll return" ("It has been done—" "Stories vary" "as to what
happens . . .") "But you will" "descend" "into an unknown" "unlit world"

"Decide" "to stay or leave" "within the next" "sixty seconds'"
"I didn't move" "The doors closed" "The lights dimmed &" "went out"
"There was no light" "within the train" "except from" "the station"
"We looked shadowy," "shadowy" "Then I felt" "my flesh tingle"

"I looked down & saw" "that my flesh" "was starting to" "disappear"
"I was becoming—" "I became—" "a shadow, literal shadow" "We"
"inside the train" "were all shadows" "But with eyes bright" "still
bright" "And then our eyes too" "became shaded" "Their moistness"

"became matte" "their whites gray" "The train began" "to pull away"

"As we pulled out" "from the platform" "there was opaqueness" "of a
tunnel" "And then a last thing," "perhaps" "a power station"
"A lit-up" "power station—" "all lightbulbs," "an erector set"
"of lightbulbs—" "it lit up little," "a few feet" "of the dark"

"The starkness" "the powerlessness" "of the electric light"
"terrified me" "Was this" "the outermost edge of" "the subway?"
"These are last lights," "we are leaving" "Train pulls away"
"Where" "are we going?" "Will I be there?" "Who am I now?"

"Going into" "true night" "endless night" "And the train,"
"has it dissolved?" "Its sides fall away" "I am floating" "There is
nothing" "but the dark" "everywhere" "around me" "And my mind"
"is still there somehow" "suddenly weightless" "I am weightless"

"Set free" "And my bit of mind" "seems to drift" "drifts in blackness"
"as on a small—" "obscurely green—" "basil leaf" "On a leaf"
"or a petal" "a piece" "of black lettuce" "Like a temple" "tiny, &
nearly" "transparent" "My mind floats" "my mind floats but"

"ever downward"

BOOK
two

"I floated" "down in darkness" "among" "the other bodiless"
"people" "from the black train" "Heard" "their whispers:" "'I feel"
"so light so empty" "of heavy thought,' they said" "'I feel" "so
unbounded'" "So we rode" "soft air" "like leaves falling" "but with

no notion" "of any" "ground to fall to—" "Then" "an old man"
"an old man's voice began" "to sing:" "'When the snake" "was the train,"
"when the snake" "was the subway, we" "entered her walking over"
"her long tongue" "her long tongue" "And inside her" "was red & white"

"& we looked out" "through clear scales" "Inside her" "was red plush,"
"was bone white" "was safe; and we" "rode her" "as she slithered"
"through the earth &" "its darkness" "through the earth &" "its dark smell
"We let" "the snake swallow us, take us into" "herself" "She had no"

"arms to hug us," "she gave us" "her whole body" "We were in"
"her whole self" "Safe in her whole self" "When a snake was" "our
mother" "When a snake was" "our train'"

"When the old man" "stopped singing" "all fell quiet," "no voices
sounded" "I lost sense of other presences," "felt nearly" "non-
existent" "Later" "I saw that" "there was a mountain," "down &"
"at a distance" "It was cone-shaped" "& shiny" "barely visible, in the

dark," "looked onyx-like" "or obsidian" "with the texture the
surface" "of a chipped-out arrowhead" "I seemed to be," "of no power of"
"my own," "headed for it" "I regretted" "having to" "arrive somewhere:"
"My smallness" "in this darkness" "had been relief &" "happiness"

"But I headed" "for the mountain" "in a gradual" "downward arc—"
"It was set in" "the most vague of" "terrains, some black flatness"
"And as I" "approached it closely," "a large eye appeared" "on the
air, an" "outline drawn in white—" "as if in scratchy" "white ink—"

"many times" "the size of" "a whole body" "There were" "lines of
character," "of humor," "beneath it" "& at its corner" "Then I
flew through" "its pupil" "And suddenly" "I had limbs again," "felt
bodied" "I landed" "before the mountain" "in a pool of" "yellow

light:" "there was a lightbulb" "in a fixture" "that projected" "from
the mountain" "Then the mountain" "shook a little," "gravel fell from it"
"The mountain opened" "in a vertical" "chasm" "A man" "was there
inside of it" "dressed like a main-" "tenance man" "He thrust out his

arm" "& pulled me inside" "Quiet, cool there, the" "smell of earth"
"protective" "& intimate—" "The wall closed" "I was within"
"a cavelike place that" "was well-lit" "I sat down on" "a boulder"
"& for no reason" "wept"

"I stood in" "a cave that was" "a sort of" "antechamber" "Its walls
were smooth, bland" "& brown" "There was a door," "a rough archway,"
"which seemed to lead towards other caves" "But I talked now" "with
the maintenance man" "He wore a navy-blue uniform" "with words
embroidered"

"in red" "on his pocket—" "they were illegible" "But what was
strangest" "was that his skin looked" "like rock like" "gray granite"
"I asked him" "what eye I" "had passed through" "in the air" "'Why
yours,'" "he said" "'Where are" "my companions?'" "'You are" "your

companions—" "your companions" "have temporarily" "become you'"
"I saw that" "my hands' outlines" "were several" "& seemed blurred"
"Likewise" "my arms & legs—" "I looked plural" "'But my eyes are"
"unified,' I said," "'my vision single," "my mind single" "Inside I

feel like" "one person'" "'Of course,'" "he said" "'That is the only way"
"to know & see," "through one person's" "mind & senses" "But in this
place," "in these depths—" "a cave network, as you will find—"
"what you see" "pertains to everyone'" "'Can you tell me" "more clearly"

"what these caves are?' I asked" "'I can't be that clear:" "But they are
something like" "our middle depths" "or middle psyche, if you prefer"
"You must pass through them" ("though not through all of them—" "by
any means") "on your way to" "your deepest origin" "Now get on with"

"your journey'" "He turned to leave me—" "I could now read" "the words"
"on his uniform" "They said, *In Use*" "'Wait a minute,' I said,"
"'can't you give me" "some directions?" "How do I" "begin?'" "'You will
simply" "begin" "through that door there—'" "he pointed" "to the

archway—" "'& pass through" "the dreams" "that are enacted" "in the
rooms . . ." "Now I really must leave'" "He walked out quickly,"
"disappeared"

"I stepped through" "the archway" "& there was" "another door"
"immediately" "before me," "another round entrance" "It led"
"into a cavern" "which was walled with" "gears & clockwork—"
"a large room," "with a rock floor," "whose walls were" "composed of"

"large round gears," "with toothed edges," "turning" "in semi-darkness—"
"the room was lit to" "twilight level:" "the gears were colored"
"blue & gray" "The round disks' surfaces" "as I looked at them" "began to
change" "to change" "Images" "appeared on them" "soon becoming" "other

images:" "patterns of small circles," "of squares &" "triangles,"
"appeared" "& dissolved" "Once" "they looked like tree-trunks, like"
"gnarled" "turning bluish wood" "Once" "they looked like flesh—"
"you could see the" "pores of skin," "which changed to" "rippled ocean,"

"then" "to dotted starry sky" "Then" "the gears were finally" "metal"
"gears again" "One gear—" "I now stood facing it—" "was larger"
"than the others" "It seemed" "to be turning" "in the center" "of my
chest" "& the enmeshing" "of its teeth" "with those of" "adjacent

gears" "produced" "sensations in me" "of deepest" "satisfaction"
"As I watched the gears" "I felt stronger," "better" "I stood there"
"a long while;" "finally I" "turned to leave" "through" "another door"

"As I went on," "a next cave" "a next entrance would" "be in front of me" "a few footsteps" "from the last one—" "But I would exit through" "a second opening" "This was the case" "throughout the caves" "Therefore" "I now entered" "without real transition," "after the room full" "of

gears," "a small cave" "in which a woman sat" "on a wooden" "folding chair—" "the room was other-" "wise empty" "She had shoulder-length dark hair," "wore a full-" "skirted cotton dress," "beige—" "'I'm a scroll-" "swallower,'" "she said to me," "'I take scripture" "on

scroll" "& hold it," "keep it in my throat—" "I've got two" "in there now but" "there's no room for" "this third one—'" "she showed me" "a roll of paper," "a small scroll—" "'What scriptures are they?'" "I asked her" "'Past, Present," "& Future—" "Oh I've got the third

one down—'" "she swallowed it—" "'Good,' she said" "'Otherwise" "I'm imperfect," "you know the way" "a baby's crazy'" "I said I didn't know" "what she meant" "'Yes," "you do,' she said" "'Once they're all down," "I wake up'" "She smiled" "& disappeared" "into the

air"

"I next approached" "a large cavern" "above the door of which" "was written" ("carved in rock") "the words *Mother Ship*" "Inside the cavern" "was a clipper ship" "its sails folded" "But the ship had" "soft-edged outlines" "& began to" "shrink & change:" "As I

came closer" "I saw that" "it was now a" "small house" "with no door on" "the hinges," "no glass, no slats in" "the windows—" "those were dark" "empty places" ("though the cave outside" "was well-lit") "They looked like two eyes" "& a nose-mouth" "'Perhaps,'" "I thought," "'it is"

"someone's head'" "Then I entered" "that dark house" "& began to" "speak aloud:" "'If this is" "the Mother Ship," "does the Mother" "have a voice?" "I call on you" "to speak to me'" "The door" "became soft &" "slightly rounded" "like gums" "The windows softened,"

"looked like flesh" "I waited" "But she couldn't seem" "to speak" "right away" "Made a sound first" "like a low wheeze" "Then the door—" "the mouth—moved" "to form" "these words" "in a whisper" "The words came slowly," "'My real voice" "is further" "further down, in"

"another place" "Keep walking" "keep walking" "I hope you finally" "get to me . . .'" "Then" "the doors & windows" "became hard-edged" "again" "The house was dirty" "inside" "There were black ants on the floor" "There was no furniture," "it was a bare" "single room" "of un-

painted" "old boards" "It made me sad," "it made me sad" "I walked out slowly"

"I entered a cave" "in which a wall" "opened back," "limitlessly—"
"like a painting" "of a landscape" "but this landscape" "was somehow
real" "It was an un-" "ending field" "that was a battleground"
"of corpses," "sometimes" "single-layered," "sometimes piled up" "in

pyramids" "The eyes" "of all the corpses" "were open" "A white
substance" "dead-white sticky," "as if spilled" "in a great spill
was everywhere," "erratically," "dripped over" "the corpses,"
"standing in the field" "in pools," "like white blood, like a thickened"

"chalky lotion" "Between myself" "& the vista—" "where the cave
wall would have been—" "was a screen" "of thinnest gauze," "almost
airy" "It was daubed" "here & there" "with the white substance"
"And there were drops of it—" "just a small trail—" "on the floor on"

"my side of" "the screen," "leading to me, it seemed," "to my feet"
"I looked down at" "my hand" "A small drop of" "this evil" "this
white substance," "oozed" "from my palm" "'I've never" "killed,'
I thought," "'I've never" "been to war" "I've never" "been allowed"

"to participate" "in the decision to go to war—'" "I then" "said
aloud," "'Who has done this to me?" "How dare he" "implicate me"
"In such evil?'" "Another white drop" "appeared" "in my hand,"
"& another" "'I've done nothing,' I said" "'Has someone" "such power"

"as to make his sin" "ooze from my pores?'" "All was quiet" "I fled
the room" "& then" "the white substance" "dried up" "disappeared from"
"my hand"

"There came to be" "a voice in" "my head" "always a faint voice"
"that ordered me" "to keep walking" "from room to room" "'Keep walking,"
"keep walking,'" "it whispered" "as I approached" "what appeared to be"
"a monstrous snake" "with a wide" "open mouth" "The snake,"

"a black snake," "which I took to be" "a female—" "she wore"
"a gold fillet" "the shape of" "delicate grasses" "& tiny flowers—"
"had black eyes" "that appeared blind," "eyes that were solid" "black
membrane," "but a pink" "flower-like mouth" "'Keep walking,'"

"the voice said," "& I entered" "her mouth," "walked among its
moist parts" "on through into" "her body's" "long dark corridor"
"Her bones were silver," "barely visible" "Made a soft noise" "like
wind chimes," "as I brushed by" "Midway" "through her body"

"I came upon" "a small alcove" "with a chair, & a lamp" "On the
chair," "chin spread" "across" "the chair's arms," "was an enormous"
"head" "of a man," "quite alive" "He had long" "shaggy hair,"
"light brown skin," "& feverish" "bloodshot eyes" "I tried" "to rush by"

"'Stop!' he said" "'You can't make me" "stop,' I said" "'But you're
inside me!'" "His voice grew louder" "'This snake is female,'" "I
answered" "'Then inside us'" "He grinned at me" "'Now worship me,"
"I am a great man!'" "'Sorry,' I said," "'I can't worship" "anything'"

"Then he squeezed" "his brows together" "angrily, &" "blew"
"a great wind at me" "I" "was carried backwards" "& blown out"
"of the snake's mouth" "I stood" "before her head again" "But she had
turned white" "all over" "Her eyes white, & her mouth" "cotton-white"

"dry &" "white as" "her fangs"

"I came upon" "a cave which" "contained" "a giant woman" "who was
lying" "on the floor" "She was ten" "or eleven" "feet tall"
"Large" "but not fat" "In a shapeless tan shift" "Normal-"
"sized people" "entered" "with clothes & trappings:" "a lace blouse,"

"flowers," "a necklace," "a red" "velvet skirt" "They helped her"
"slip the clothes on—" "she was slow," "inattentive" "The flowers
were a" "crown" "for her head of" "matted dark hair" "Then someone
crowned her" "& said," "'She is now made," "she can give birth'"

"The giantess" "remained impassive" "Then they left the room"
"She reached" "beneath her skirt," "between her legs," "& pulled out"
"the baby" "As she cradled it" "& cradled it" "the trappings"
"fell from her" "The chaplet" "of flowers" "disappeared" "Her clothes

dissolved" "She could be seen" "to be alternately" "herself & a"
"blurred naked man" "who was also" "the mother—" "he was" "the
same mother" "the same body" "as she," "cradling" "the baby"
"His face" "became clearer" "It was round;" "his mouth was wide"

"He had cropped hair," "distant eyes—" "a pale-gray to her"
"raisin-dark ones" "Suddenly" "he separated" "himself from" "the
giantess" "Stood" "apart from her" "from her &" "the baby"
"And she had shrunk" "had shrunk instantly" "to a normal-" "sized

woman" "'Now,' he said," "'that we are separate," "I am the larger"
"I am the taller" "Now that I" "am separate," "I can be stronger"
"I am clear'" "Then the man" "& the woman" "both turned to me"
"& asked," "'Is this true?" "Is this what happened" "a long time

ago?'" "'I don't know,'" "I said" "Then the room filled" "with a
dark mist" "a cold mist" "They were gone" "I was alone"

"There was a cave in which," "when I entered it," "I rose up in air"
"to hover" "against the ceiling" "looking down at" "the floor"
"The floor was" "a movie screen" "on which was shown" "a desert"
"in daytime, sandy white" "with bare cactus trees," "leafless tree forms"

"light brown & faintest green" "There were" "distant mountains,"
"a pale sky" "above them" "But there were hundreds" "of these trees,"
"close together," "at regular intervals" "They were short &"
"all alike" "But one—" "just one—" "which I felt I" "was meant to

look at—" "was larger," "that was all," "somewhat larger"
"Indifference," "sadness," "a perfunctory" "sort of interest" "were"
"what I felt" "A dark" "male presence," "a rather bodiless" "man,"
"came & hovered" "beside me" " 'If the larger tree,' he said," " 'were

you, say," "or I," "would it make" "any difference?' " " 'Not really,'
I said" " 'Or it would,' he said," " 'change the landscape," "a little,"
"the way it looks' " " 'But to whom?' I said" " 'To those who hover"
"above it?" "Larger of same" "in that landscape" "is nothing anyway' "

" 'Forget it,' he said," " 'it's just something" "to look at' "

"I came upon" "a group of people," "ten or so," "relaxed &
sitting" "on boulders," "in a cave" "They had red eyes," "entirely
red—" "red pupils, red whites—" "red-light red," "stained-glass
red" "A man whose profile" "seemed familiar" "turned to face me,

& said," "'We are waiting" "to cross the river," "are you the pilot"
"of the boat?'" "'No,' I said, "'but" "why are" "your eyes so red?'"
"'We're dead; we're demon-saints;" "it is hard for us" "to get across"
"the river'" "'What river?'" "'We don't" "exactly know yet'" "'What

is a demon-saint?' I asked" "'Drink from this paper cup" "& find out'"
"It contained" "a black liquor that" "had a hint of red" "phosphorescence"
"'It will make you be like us," "temporarily," "make your eyes red
for a time'" "I began to see" "through a red film" "& to feel strange"

"sensations:" "as if" "I had killed," "killed many people," "the way a
soldier has," "has fought & killed" "for others" "Sadness" "& hysteria"
"made my heart expand" "into an" "immense" "sick flower" "grotesque
blossom" "huge red orchid," "with an attenuated thin" "yellow stem"

"which couldn't drink in" "enough moisture" "I danced I ran" "about the
room" "as if to make the" "flower smaller" "'That is a strange dance,'"
"the man said," "'which I recognize'" "I danced until" "the drug
wore off:" "my feet had beat" "a curving line," "a narrow trench into"

"the rock floor" "'It will hold water,'" "the man said," "'it will be
deep enough," "when the water comes" "We will be able" "to cross'"
"I fell asleep," "exhausted" "& when I woke up" "the red-eyed people"
"were gone &" "the narrow trench" "was also gone," "the floor was"

"smooth again"

"A large cavern contained" "the skeleton of a" "colossal woman"
"On the skull was" "a wig & crown," "the wig" "long & coarse brown—"
"& not ancient;" "the shiny crown—" "also" "new-looking—"
"set with" "flat blue lapis" "I stepped into" "the skeleton's

huge ribcage," "stood where" "the heart had been" "'Going further,"
"going further,'" "I heard a faint" "woman's voice say," "'Going
backwards," "going backwards" "in time'" "'Am I closer?' I asked"
"'Can you speak yet?" "Are you our mother?'" "A firefly appeared"

"in the center" "of the ribcage" "It floated vibrantly" "before me"
"& seemed to be" "the source of" "her voice:" "'I was" "a queen,'
she said," "'before they banished me" "beneath the earth" "made me"
"a serpent . . .'" "'I'm not looking for" "a queen,' I said" "'A

queen is not" "my origin" "Our mother would not" "be a mother"
"of others' poverty," "a mother" "of the subway—" "You are
not her" "are not her'" "The firefly's" "light went out;" "I
left the cave"

"I entered" "a soft cave," "soft to the touch, like flesh"
"Inside this room" "my clothes evaporated" "from my body—" "I was
now" "all flesh," "soft as the walls" "The air" "in this room was"
"peculiarly soft too" "There was a bed against one wall" "I sat

down on it" "A naked man appeared," "suddenly," "to sit beside me"
"He smiled" "& said," "'I wonder" "what it's like" "not" "to have
a sex'" "'I believe that in this room" "we can find out,' I said"
"'Let's give" "our sex organs" "to these" "fleshy walls'" "'How

can we do that?' he asked" "'I believe,' I said," "'they will disattach,"
"though I don't know" "how I know this'" "We disattached them then—"
"my vagina," "his penis" "Pulled them out of" "our bodies" "like
rocks stuck into clay—" "& inserted them" "shallowly" "in the

cave walls," "where they stayed fast" "And then all at once" "I
couldn't see," "see anything" "except vaguely" "a brown-pink flesh tint"
"I seemed to swim in it," "ride waves of it" "uncontrollably"
"I couldn't think" "at all" "Was formless," "was in chaos" "The man

cried, 'I've become lost'" "And I too" "shrieked out to him" "somehow,"
"that my mind was becoming lost," "unfocused," "stretched out & thin—"
"I saw it as" "black water" "oily black" "a slimy puddle" "hung in air &"
"spreading vertically" "thinly" "over the brown-pink tint . . ." "'I want"

"my sex back!' I screamed" "My sex" "was then replaced" "between my
legs," "instantly back" "The man's" "was too;" "& we were then
delineated," "formed," "ourselves again"

"I saw a tree" "in blackness" "a leafless tree hung with" "grinning heads" "The faces" "were dead-white," "made up clownlike," "with white face paint" "& red lipstick smiles" "I knew instantly" "these were the heads of" "the soon-to-die" "I seemed to recognize" "one or

two" "from somewhere," "from the subway," "& know them" "to be suffering" "from slow" "self-destruction" "or extreme lives:" "drugs," "danger," "aftermath" "of war," "emotional" "extremity" "Their smiles were huge," "on the trees, their" "humanity all gone in"

"the bizarre paint" "I thought to run to" "another room, then" "stood still instead" "Stood & stared back at the heads" "hung on a wintry" "black tree" "in a black cave" "One of the heads" "began to speak to me" "It was a man with" "long orange hair" "His mouth grinned

as he spoke:" "'If you are frightened" "if you are frightened," "then stand &" "be frightened" "For you will die too," "you will die," "if not so garishly" "as I'" "Then fear came" "in electric waves," "fear of losing" "my 'I'," "fear of personal" "extinction" "I

fell to" "the floor," "moaned a little," "hugged myself" "The tree remained" "The heads remained" "The tree would not change" "or go away" "There was nothing" "to do" "but gain control of" "myself" "I stood up," "stared at the tree" "of death" "once more" "Then I left"

"I stood before" "3 paintings" "painted onto cave walls," "faded,"
"partly effaced" "One was a portrait" "of the tyrant" "in white,"
"pink, & blue—" "white-haired pale man" "He looked noble," "deeply
serious" "Swaths of rock showed" "across his face & chest" "through

the worn-" "away paint" "Close by" "was a nude" "standing woman"
"She had no face" "but where her face should be" "was a black hole"
"which tunneled back" "behind the wall" "The third painting" "was the
face of" "an animal," "a mountain lion," "yellow-brown—" "its paint

fading" "overall" "The paintings" "were disappearing" "as I
stood there" "Paint dissolving," "rock encroaching" "faster & faster,"
"as if time were" "speeded up in" "this room" "I began to weep—"
"a pressure" "from this speeding-up" "of time" "seemed to squeeze

tears" "from my eyes" "I wasn't" "sad inside," "but I wept & wept"
"A roaring" "sucking wind" "began blowing" "all around me" "The room
darkened;" "I stood suddenly" "inside the" "painted woman,"
"stood nude inside" "her dark facelessness:" "I had" "become her,"

"& the tunnel" "behind her face" "was now life-size," "was what I
stood in" "just behind the" "wall of paintings" "The tyrant's portrait"
"came alive & spoke" "'Don't walk through" "the tunnel" "At the end of
it" "you will die" "Look at me," "see how I'm truly" "afraid for you'"

"'But I can't see you,'" "I said viciously," "'I have" "no face'"
"I did" "have sight, but" "where I stood was" "very dark" "I began"
"to walk further" "into the tunnel" "'This tunnel" "represents"
"my whole journey, doesn't it?'" "—I called back to" "the tyrant—"

"'Well I'm going to" "see it through'" "Then I saw floating" "in air,"
"coming towards me," "a real lion's face," "bristly, moist-eyed—"
"I feared it might" "attack me:" "instead it fastened" "itself" "onto
the blackness above my neck—" "it gave me its face" "I took several"

"more steps forward," "but at that point" "the tunnel vanished"
"I stood outside" "the cave of paintings" "I touched my face:" "it was
my own" "& I was" "clothed again," "was back in" "my real journey"
"In front of me" "lay the next door" "I must pass through"

“I entered” “a cave” “in which I instantly” “divided into three”
“separate” “figures,” “chained together” “in single file”
“I was most the one” “in the middle” “A man stood watching us,”
“professorial,” “in glasses, bearded,” “dressed in suit & tie”

“ ‘Why are there three of me” “in here?’ I—we—asked him,” “our voices
separate,” “out of sync” “ ‘You are your” “Past, Present,” “& Future,’
he said” “ ‘You divide into” “those components” “in this room’ ”
“ ‘But I do not have” “components!’ ” “our three voices said,” “ ‘My

secret name—” “Time’s secret name—” “is Oneness,” “is One Thing’ ”
“As I—the one” “in the middle—spoke,” “the one of us in front—”
“who was the Past—” “had already” “finished speaking” “& was awaiting”
“his reply” “He said,” “ ‘Don’t we seem” “to experience” “things

somewhat this way?” “There *is* past, present” “& future’ ” “The Future
then cried out,” “ ‘Where is my life?” “Where is my life?” “You have
stolen” “my life!’ ” “There was a silence” “The man” “reached out &”
“pressed a button” “on the cave wall—” “we three united” “into

one again” “while he wrote words on” “a clipboard” “Then he looked up
& said,” “ ‘Going forward?” “Going on?” “Death lies ahead, you know’ ”
“ ‘Any woman” “may already” “be dead,’ ” “I said” “ ‘What do you mean?’
he asked” “I opened” “my lips, but” “someone else seemed” “to speak,”

“ ‘No remembrance” “No remembrance.” “No remembrance” “of our mother”
“No remembrance” “of who we really are” “Thus a woman” “may be”
“already dead” “born dead’ ”

"I entered" "a cave" "whose walls closed up" "around me," "until"
"it became" "exactly my size, my body's size" "I stood & stood there"
"stood forever" "A small" "blue salamander" "came out from" "beneath a
rock" "He was turquoise blue," "clear like jelly" "I couldn't move well"

"move freely;" "but he climbed up to" "my shoulder," "sometimes peered
into"
"my face" "He had a tiny face" "with a black-line mouth," "tiny black"
"eyes with whites" "Occasionally" "as I stood there" "I would feel"
"something like" "an orgasmic" "sensation," "a hollow shiver—"

"not exactly from" "the salamander," "but from no one," "from nowhere"
"The sensation" "had a visual" "manifestation" "as thin frond shapes"
"etched in gray," "trembling in the air" "in front of me" "While I was
in this space," "when I looked down" "at my arms & hands" "they weren't

plural" "Instead," "a clear single edge" "delineated them" "I
became sad" "sadder . . ." "Until" "I fell asleep:" "& dreamed of falling"
"from a mountain" "high as an airplane" "to a blue map" "in darkness"
"I fell onto—" "the map became—" "a field of" "snow at night"

"cold & cleansing" "pure & cold" "When I woke up" "my room was larger,"
"had a door &" "I was plural," "was others," "was my companions" "again"

"In a dark cave, I saw" "an apparition:" "almost real, almost there—"
"a human-sized" "hooded snake," "which looked as if" "it had arms"
"wing arms" "cape arms" "The snake" "had a smiling" "womanly face"
"Reared up taller than I" "Seemed to hold towards me arms" "Then

vanished" "the cave lightened" "grew full of light—" "but also" "seemed
curiously" "buoyant" "I felt light-footed;" "the air itself" "was
balmy" "Other" "people entered now" "who were naked or" "half-clad"
"Then I saw" "a black line" "begin extending in air—" "in the center"

"of the room—" "made an" "airy drawing," "rectangular," "six feet tall"
"'That is *The Senses,*'" "a woman said," "'Step through it, it's a door'"
"I stepped through the" "rectangle" "& immediately the walls" "of the
cave" "looked different" "They were covered" "with jewels" "But the

jewels were" "cartoon jewels—" "as if from" "an animated" "cartoon—
& more beautiful" "than real jewels" "Larger," "the colors clearer,"
"brighter," "more transparent" "Everything" "about them was" "magical"
"Their colors were" "white-glinty violet" "bright orange" "magenta"

"blood red" "fierce blue" "green-spotted black . . ." "'These are the ones,'"
"a voice said," "'We've always wanted" "to be near'" "It was" "a man
who spoke" "We sat down together" "on the cave floor," "in shadows,"
"bright jewels" "all about us," "& began to make love" "Part of me"

"seemed to float above" "our bodies" "& I saw that" "we looked like
cartoons," "outlined in black," "drawn & painted" "But as we made love"
"we changed to" "thick velvety black air" "Blackness" "flowing out,"
"rayed from" "a small center," "another jewel," "clear yellow—"

"which was" "the point" "where our" "sexes met . . ." "Afterwards,"
"the man fell asleep" "I left the room," "resumed walking" "'Keep
walking," "keep walking,'" "the voice was saying" "in my head"

"I entered" "a cavern" "in which a queen sat" "on a throne—"
"a golden woman," "metallic woman, in" "black-yarn wig" "& gold crown,"
"kohl-outlined eyes" "The queen" "was being bowed to" "by white-robed
figures;" "the floor before the throne" "was strewn with" "plastic

petals" "As I watched her" "she grew larger," "grew taller" "& also
fatter—" "expanded like" "a balloon" "Until" "with a loud bang" "she
exploded," "disappeared" "Her courtiers" "vanished into air" "& Where"
"the throne had been," "sat a woman, on the ground," "weaving straw into"

"a basket" "I approached her & sat down" "She was dark-robed" "& dark-
eyed" "She lifted towards me" "the half-made basket," "& I pressed my"
"cheek to it" "It was smooth & tight" "& tan" "It gave off" "a dull
light" "whose very mutedness" "was its beauty" "I sat quietly"

"there a long time," "as she resumed" "her weaving" "Watched her
hands weave" "the straw" "Until I realized" "I had become" "the basket"
"in her hands—" "looked out" "from where the basket was:" "no one
sat now" "where I had sat" "I had no wish to be" "otherwise" "A creek

was running" "in the cave, & I" "listened" "to the water" "as she
handled me" "as she wove me" "When the basket" "was completed"
"I became my" "human self," "sat across from her," "again, but" "the
basket" "now had a stripe" "broad, single stripe" "of red" "It was

my blood, thick" "& caked" "Dull red," "drying red," "it was"
"my own blood"

"I entered" "a dark cave" "stood in a lightless cave room"
"Could see nothing" "at all" "Then my body" "dissolved," "until
I was" "a single small thing" "a cell of 'I' afloat" "on the
dark air" "'Am I still" "the others," "my companions?' I asked aloud"

"'You are us still,'" "I heard voices say" "'This I,'" "I thought,"
"'isn't so small'" "I felt curious," "humorous," "quite poised"
"despite my size" "And those feelings" "seemed to work a change"
"on the darkness:" "a jagged" "turquoise line" "shot out from me"

"& unfurled downward" "into a sheet of" "white light" "like an airy"
"movie screen" "& then I saw" "on that quasi-screen" "this scene:"
"A group of people stood" "naked crowded" "on a small island"
"in the ocean" "All was early blue" "blue sky & water" "White flesh was

bluish," "dark flesh had blue glints" "I saw that" "I was one of"
"those people—" "& now I entered" "that scene," "my reality"
"was on the island" "And one of us" "was a murderer" "He held a gun"
"down by his side," "his face was desolate," "made old" "I walked to"

"the water's edge" "& looked down into" "the water" "I saw there"
"a strange mermaid a" "girl child" "with tangled black hair" "who had a
man's" "hairy chest" "& a fish's" "lower body" "Her scales were dark,"
"emerald-black" "I poked my head beneath" "the water," "'Who are you?'

"I asked in a" "bubbling" "underwater way" "She answered quite clearly,"
"in a slightly" "childish voice," "'A forgotten" "possibility" "You,"
"you yourself," "don't want my" "hairy chest now" "Your people" "have
divided" "themselves in two:" "have made" "domination" "your principle:"

"why have you done this?'" "'I don't know,' I said," "'how it happened"
"What I like of yours" "is your streamlined" "leglessness" "Your human
qualities" "make me sad'" "'But you must not,' she said," "'hate
creation . . ." "must not . . ." "You must begin again," "create again"

"each moment . . .'" "Suddenly" "I couldn't breathe, I was" "drowning"
"I fought to rise" "to the surface" "When I finally did" "I stood again"
"in a dark empty cave" "I had my body" "was back" "I left the room"

"I opened" "a door to" "a dark desert," "nighttime-like desert,"
"in a cave:" "It was both there &" "depicted" "Both reality—"
"vast—" "& a movie" "on the walls of" "a room" "Its colors"
"were dark & red," "brown & black," "harsh" "Sometimes" "glaring

light" "poured in to open up" "the darkness" "Soon the edges"
"of the room" "began to" "teem with figures" "Dark-clothed people"
"swathed in cloth" "walking" "beside horses—" "I sensed horses"
"in the shadows" "And then I was" "one of those people" "It was the

past or" "the future" "We were" "a horde of nomads" "of migrants"
"after a war or" "revolution" "Our hearts—" "my heart—" "I could
see into" "my own chest" "as if from" "a distance—" "contained a
picture of" "forest stubble," "blackened tree stumps" "Our babies"

"cried dirty tears" "Our leaders" "were all men;" "our women's
hands" "worked with" "meal & water" "I was imprisoned in" "my heart &
clothes" "I walked with" "greater" "& greater difficulty . . ."
"Till my entire" "my entire" "body" "burst open" "like a seam"

"seam splitting" "from screaming mouth" "to crotch" "Blood burst
out of me" "in slow motion—" "I watched this" "as it happened—"
"& also" "from inside me" "came a black sprite" "small winged thing"
"Winged," "but couldn't leave them," "winged" "but stayed & hovered"

"about the nomads," "flew near them" "as they continued on" "after
burying" "my body"

"I found," "in a cavern," "a huge black crystal" "shot with red;"
"the size of" "a cubicle," "hollowed out &" "with a door"
"As I neared the door" "I saw that" "a figure stood inside" "this
darkly" "red place" "this immense" "black-red garnet—" "she stood"

"in its center," "with a low sink" "in front of her—" "a woman,"
"a dark-skinned woman," "with eyes closed," "working with" "something
claylike" "She seemed both clothed" "& naked," "for I could see through"
"her clothes" "Her genitals" "were blank, were not there—" "As her

eyes were" "large smooth eyelids," "did not open," "in fact" "Her hands
were working," "were engaged in" "a making, a" "shaping," "a playing
with a" "dark" "oozing moist mass in the sink" "She squeezed & kneaded it,"
"let it slip through" "her fingers" "Let it drip down like mud—"

"All" "the while she hummed" "a song with" "an always-changing" "shape,
un-" "repeatable:" "Suddenly" "she held up a" "statue," "small,"
"powerfully simple," "a hairless," "sexless figure" "Just as quickly"
"it wasn't there, was mud again—" "She laughed &" "continued" "to work:"

"Had she" "somehow seen it?" "I" "couldn't tell; but she knew"
"that I stood there" "& she said to me:" "'Staying" "is the making,"
"the real making'" "Then after" "a while" "she held up something else:"
"a globe, a" "mappemonde" "with mud continents but" "blue seas"

"of literal" "water:" "it sloshed about" "on the globe—" "which she
held carefully," "by the poles, with fingertips—" "'Does it look like it?'"
"'I guess,' I said" "'What's" "the point?' she said" "'I was about to
ask you'" "'That's the last thing" "a god would know,' she said"

"'Are you" "a god?' I asked" "'I don't know, I" "don't know'" "She
laughed again" "& then she" "& the whole jewel" "dissolved"

"In a cavern" "there was a small stream" "& I sat down" "beside it
tired" "I saw across the stream," "cut into the wall," "a door that"
"was a slab of rock" "It opened—" "bright yellow light" "streamed from
behind it," "& a man whom" "at first I couldn't see" "emerged"

"Then he stepped closer," "focused on me" "I saw that" "he was the
tyrant" "He had curl today" "in his white hair," "smiled boyishly at me,"
" 'Would you like" "to come inside" "& rest" "on a real bed?' " "I saw
a bed" "beyond the door," "with clean bedding" "& big pillows" " 'No

thank you,' I said" "He smiled again," "then a small image" "of the
door—" "three inches high—" "appeared" "before my feet,"
"& leaped up" "onto my forehead" "I was now" "as if dreaming,"
"was in a fantasy" "in my own mind" "I uncontrollably approached the

door—" "the tyrant" "was no longer near—" "& entered" "the room"
"It was full of" "food & drink:" "wine & apples," "bread & cheeses,"
"berries," "unbruised lettuce," "pink ham &" "thin-sliced beef"
"But there was something" "already" "in the bed, a" "strange form:"

"Human" "without facial features," "without eyes," "nose or mouth"
"Nude & reddish-colored," "wizening" "wizening before my eyes—"
"its unsensed face shrinking," "its emaciated" "torso shrinking,"
"changing," "rotting . . ." " 'He is a corpse" "from a battlefield,'

a voice said," " 'He's just" "a dead soldier" "We will remove him
from your bed' " "The man who spoke—" "an attendant" "to the tyrant—"
"now approached" "with a shovel" "But I left" "left the room"
"& tried to" "cross the stream" ("It was only" "about a foot wide) I"

"couldn't" "move my legs" "except a little" "just a little . . ." "I
awoke then" "where I had been," "on the other side" "of the stream,"
"weeping" "for the man," "the dead soldier," "in the bed"

"I entered" "a cave" "where a woman sat" "who looked made of rock—"
"had gray granite-like skin," "though her eyes" "were lucid gray-green"
"She was clearly" "grieving for" "a man," "lifeless near her,"
"lying on the ground" "Tears ran over her rock face" "'Your son?' I asked—"

"his face was like hers—" "though not rocklike" "She nodded"
"'How shall" "we celebrate this?' I said," "not knowing" "exactly why"
"I said 'celebrate'—" "I seemed meant to" "'We'll carve" "his name,'
she said," "'into a wall" "where there are so" "many names" "that

none" "remains legible" "for very long" "All the carved names" "together"
"make a texture" "much more beautiful" "& mysterious" "than even"
"stone itself" "Then we'll" "commit his body" "to" "the deeper
darkness," "deepest darkness'" "'And what of you?' I asked," "'how will

you be?'" "She smiled" "& said," "'I am" "of course rock" "I'm
afraid" "I have" "turned to rock'"

"I entered a cave" "which was all white inside" "& smooth & round in"
"a regular way" "I was beneath" "a white dome," "& on the white floor"
"were scores of" "what seemed to be" "serpentine" "shadows—" "small,
black," "& nebulous," "a mass of almost-snakes" "A voice," "disembodied

"spoke to me:" "'This cave,' it said—" "or she said," "a female voice—"
"'is like a snake egg" "Lie down on" "the floor" "among these ghostly
snake babies'" "Then I lay down" "& wriggled with them:" "pressed my
arms to"
"my side," "my legs together—" "I laughed doing so" "'Now close your eye

the voice said" "I closed my eyes" "& was no longer" "playing snake in"
"a cave:" "I was" "a snakelike line" "on an ocean somewhere," "but was
not even" "quite a line" "I was a ripple," "not quite defined" "I was
a line that would not" "quite form," "that floated," "flowed out"

"Below me" "the ocean" "was ab-" "solutely empty," "full of light but
lifeless" "Its floor was bare & flat" "Peaceful," "it was peaceful,"
"to be almost" "a line" "Soon the voices said," "'You must open"
"your eyes" "Resume your journey" "Keep walking" "keep walking" "You c

"have legs" "Time for you" "proceeds step-by-step," "yet there is"
"something snakelike" "in your journey's" "movement" "You have not
lost her," "you have not lost her" "You bring things with you" "much
faster" "than step" "by step" "But keep walking" "Keep walking'"

"I entered, this time," "a long corridor," "in which I soon felt"
"that I" "was being followed" "I turned" "to look behind—" "a figure
vanished" "whom I just glimpsed," "a woman" "darkly robed"
"A minute later" "I saw her" "ahead of me," "where the path turned"

"& rose higher," "led to a door with" "a torch outside" "She
went in there" "& I soon followed" "I" "was now inside" "a great
chamber," "empty dark" "She sat alone" "in its center" "beside a fire"
"She was the woman" "who had woven me" "into a basket," "had decorated"

"a basket" "with my blood:" "She had olive skin," "a thin-lipped"
"smiling" "knowing mouth—" "the lines" "on her face" "of a woman"
"in her forties" "I approached her" "'What is your story?' I asked"
"'I made you,' she answered" "'I know that you" "are my history,"

"but why" "do you follow me?'" "'To tell you this:" "There are few
books" "by us," "by women," "because it wasn't" "to be books"
"It was to be" "something else:" "the same instant" "of life forever"
("Perhaps like" "an insect's" "bright being," "or an animal's")

"Books" "books ruined us" "Scrolls & tablets" "created time," "created"
"keeping track" "Distanced us from the" "perpetuation" "of our
beautiful" "beginning moment . . . " "only moment" "Created death" "created
death," "death being" "the child of men'" "'You are too" "well spoken,'

I said," "'& so" "I can't believe you," "exactly'" "Then she" "appeared
angry" "& changed suddenly" "into a crow" "with red & blue gleams"
"in black feathers" "& a yellow" "beak that glowed" "in the firelight:"
"'However,' she said," "'it may have happened," "we all lost" "our

moment" "Our moment" "of life" "No one" "has lived" "for thousands"
"of years'" "She flew up" "into the shadows" "of the ceiling &"
"disappeared" "I myself" "was shaken" "I didn't" "believe her" "Not
exactly—" "but I was shaken"

"I entered a cave" "full of women in" "black clothes, long-skirted,"
"their heads covered" "They surrounded" "a woman" "in a light
shapeless shift—" "who stood weeping" " 'What has happened?' " "I
asked one of them" "in a whisper" " 'She is a widow,' was the answer,"

" 'Her husband has just died:" "watch & see" "what happens now' "
"Slowly, the woman" "sank to the floor," "as if sorrowfully" "dancing"
"As if the air were" "a weight which" "pressed" "her body down"
"First she sat" "with her knees up" "& as she sat, her skin" "began to

turn gray" "gray & grainy" "It turned" "into rock," "though her eyes"
"were still moist" "Then she—" "again, slowly—" "lay down on her side,"
"her back curved," "her legs drawn up," "her knees close to" "her breasts"
"She laid one arm" "on the floor" "encircling her head—" "the other

made a" "semicircle" "in front of" "her breasts" "All curves"
"& hills, she" "became" "herself cavelike" "She froze" "into a model of"
"caves like the caves" "we stood in" "Her facial features disappeared"
"Her garment turned to rock" "She was caves" "she was caves" "I was

now afraid I stood" "exactly" "inside of" "women's bodies:" "Was"
"the human psyche" "made of women" "turned to stone? . . . "

"In a cave I saw" "a film projected" "onto a rock wall," "which
showed a naked" "woman & man" "moving slowly" "among greenness,"
"trees & shrubs" "Others like them" "soon appeared," "& these words
were superimposed" "upon the scene:" "*The First Ones*" "I understood

by that" "that these were the first" "people ever" "Then I forgot"
"which two I'd seen first," "tried to remember," "but I couldn't"
"Nor could I" "remember" "the faces" "of any others, from moment" "to
moment—" "I would try" "but I'd forget" "I'd think, 'Ah this one,"

"I'm fixing this one" "in memory' " "A moment later" "I wouldn't know"
"which one that" "had been" "They were" "as alike for me" "as leaves on"
"a tree;" "their movements leisurely," "pure & beautiful" "They often"
"fell into twos, into couples" "Children" "appeared among them" "Had they

been there" "from the beginning?" "I couldn't" "quite recall"
"Then a woman" "lay down" "on the ground &" "fell asleep" "Her dream
appeared" "above her head," "that there was" "a blue shape," "vertical,"
"amoeboid—" "a pool" "of blue" "Nearby" "a thick brown line" "began

extending" "from a point in air—" "to the left of" "the blue shape,"
"but in a plane" "in front of it" "It moved straight towards" "the
blue shape," "approached it & pierced it through" "Extended out from it"
"on the other side" "The dream dissolved" "The woman" "had blood on"

"her chest" "She was dead," "killed by the dream," "as far as" "I
could tell" "The words" "*First Murder*" "appeared" "onscreen" "Then a
rectangle" "of light" "which disappeared"

"I found" "a room of voices" "It was a cave of" "small containers"
"urns" "glass bottles" "rusted coffee cans" "old alembics—"
"each" "contained a voice" "which emerged in" "a line of white smoke"
"& spoke" "in midair" "When I entered" "the cave," "the air was

voices" "entangled," "a snarl a blur of" "white smoke" "They seemed"
"to be voices" "of direction to action" "or even," "to emotion:"
" 'eat some meat' " " 'you can cry now' " " 'the pain" "is overwhelming' "
" 'if you make love," "you will find it' " " 'in two days" "you will

find it' " " 'Go to sleep' " " 'Sing a funny song' " " 'Find something"
"you can worship' " " 'Cross the room' " " 'Lie down' " " 'Kill the tyrant' "
" 'Cross the river . . . ' " "Phrases" "were repeated," "almost sung,
choruslike" "I stood still in their midst" "while they noised" "all

around me" "There was a larger" "container" "sunk into" "the ground"
"like a well" "It was a black urn" "& its voice arose" "in a grayer
smoke" "It spoke" "in a rich" "female whisper:" " 'Don't guard"
"your footsteps" "Don't guard" "your footsteps" "I will protect you"

"I always do" "Don't" "protect yourself, I" "will protect you"
"while you pay me" "no mind' " "There were gold sparks" "in the gray
smoke" "I tried" "to catch one," "like an insect," "between my thumb &"
"middle finger" "but it instantly" "became invisible—" " 'Whose voices

are you?' " "I asked them all" " 'Voices" "voices of" "whoever's here"
"voices here" "You are the mind of" "our voices" "What else would"
"you like us" "to say?" "Tell us the next thing" "to say' " "I said,
'I want you" "to say," " '*Whatever*" "*is frozen*" "*will now melt*' "

" 'It will melt" "it will melt now" "will melt,' they" "began to chorus"
" 'Whatever's frozen" "will now melt . . . ' " "I slipped out of" "the room"

"I entered" "a vast cavern—" "barely lit by flickering" "lights"
"like stars" "in the black of the" "unseen ceiling" "The cavern's
central floor" "was ice," "a frozen pond" "I stepped out onto"
"its middle area" "The ice was" "like a diamond," "hard & shiny—"

"clear" "You could see into it" "& inside it" "I saw a"
"frozen face" "Was it perhaps" "my own?" "A face of" "a woman"
"who was suspended" "in the ice" "Light eyes & dark hair," "hair fanning
outward" "like a fresh-" "water weed" "Her eyes were" "imploring,"

"stared at me" "frozen gray" "I was fascinated" "by the clarity"
"of the outline" "of her body:" "dark hair & eyelash" "gray iris"
"ragged fingernails" "bulge of wristbone—" "she held her hands up"
"as if trying" "to push out of" "the ice" "I heard footsteps" "on the

pond" "A man joined me" "& said," "'The ice will melt now" "The
switch is on'" "Instantly" "the ice was water," "except for"
"floes we stood on" "The woman beneath the ice" "rushed upwards"
"to the surface" "She climbed atop a" "third floe," "wet & panting,"

"long hair streaming" "We three floated" "to the pond's édge &"
"stepped onto" "a still-hard surface," "which extended around" "the room's
periphery" "'Who are you?'" "I asked her" "She said, lips trembling,"
"'. . . frozen soul," "was dormant soul . . ." "I cannot yet" "speak well,"

"I'm still cold'" "She vanished" "through the exit door" "'Does she
look like me?'" "I asked the man" "'Yes,'" "he said," "'I think she's
very much like you" "I think she" "might be you'"

"I entered" "a cavern" "& immediately" "felt a fluttering"
"of something inside my shirt—" "a sinister" "tickling:"
"A small" "mothlike bat" "flew out of" "my shirt," "up my
back &" "out the shirt's neck" "I felt" "other bats now" "My

back was brushed by" "their fleshy wings" "I was panicked:" "saw
vaguely" "at one end of" "the cavern," "& as high as it," "some
sort of" "black & red" "mask," "floating" "before a darkness—"
"no rock wall" "behind it" "The bats—" "there were several—"

"struggled out of my shirt," "flew towards the mask" "& into its"
"black sense holes—" "disappeared" "I approached" "the mask then,"
"sank to the floor" "before it" "Its material" "seemed to be"
"brocade-like:" "It consisted of" "red roses" "embossed on"

"transparent plastic," "through which was visible" "the vibrant
darkness" "behind the mask" "The mask thus" "appeared to be"
"composed of roses" ("themselves the size of" "human faces")
"floating" "on a face shape" "made of air," "made of black night"

"The roses" "were sumptuous," "soft, & yet," "slightly waxen"
"as if red paraffin" "had been lightly—" "almost" "imperceptibly—"
"brushed over them" "The darkness behind the mask" "was an emptiness"
"I could see nothing in" "Yet all of this—" "mask & voice behind—"

"seemed alive," "electric," "the mask a" "sort of deity—" "some
divine" "neuter principle" "I felt love &" "awe for it"
"Or rather" "its lush roses" "seemed to" "become" "my feelings of
love & awe" "And then, of course," "it dissolved," "the mask

dissolved" "A brown rock panel" "slid over the" "airy void"
"I was returned to" "the plainness" "of the cavern," "stood up
again" "to go &" "find another"

"I entered" "a cave" "which was empty" "except for" "a rather
small snake" "on the floor," "perhaps a foot long," "brown
& plain" "It slid towards me," "lifted up its head—" "it had
spare black friendly features," "dot eyes & linear mouth—" "& said"

"in a high-pitched" "but sexless, amusing voice:" "'A snake is"
"just a snake" "A snake has snake toys," "knows snake songs," "& is"
"a snake . . . '" "'May I ask you" "a question?" "since you are here,'
"I said" "The snake nodded" "'What is" "the divine" "neutral

principle?" "do you know?—" "since what these caves do" "is know;"
"& you are in one'" "'Well,' the snake said," "'a snake" "has a
snake god" "Not neutral," "it is scaly," "though I guess it has no
sex" "& that's all I know'" "'Then are you,' I asked," "'a clue to"

"the woman" "I'm looking for?" "A lost" "first mother," "an Eve
unlike Eve," "or anyone" "whose name we know'" "'A depiction"
"of me,' the snake said," "'will help you find her," "when the time comes"
"Oracularly speaking," "my symbol will mark her place" "And some

may say" "I am her—" "Obviously I'm not" "Remember me here,"
"when you can, when" "you want to laugh" "Humor" "is closer" "to the
divine than" "you might think" "The trouble is" "when you're laughing"
"you don't always" "bother with" "anything" "else," "like thinking,"

"like helping" "Excuse me I have to go" "I must return to" "the
snake world . . . '" "It then" "disappeared," "leaving behind a" "molted
snakeskin" "that evaporated into" "a pile of dust" "with a faint"
"stinky odor" "which made" "me laugh"

"I entered a cave in which" "there was a mirror" "across one wall"
"A man stood" "before it—" "I saw the back of his" "dark-haired head"
"But in the mirror" "his image" "was a shapeless" "gray substance,"
"thin sticky-looking," "gummy" "As I came towards" "the mirror"

"a similar image" "appeared beside his" "that was obviously mine"
" 'What does this mirror show?' I asked" " 'I'm not sure,' he said"
"In the act of" "conversing" "we seemed to" "have made" "the two
images" "slide close together" "& merge, in one place," "their

irregular" "borders" "I then walked away from him" "to see what"
"would happen" "The substance" "was so sticky," "that when my image"
"pulled away from his," "bits of my" "gray substance" "stayed attached to"
"his gray substance;" "& mine took on" "a frayed look" "where I

"had broken loose" " 'I suppose,' I said," " 'we exchange it" "with
others" "all the time' " " 'It doesn't seem to be" "individualized,'
he said" "Then he left the room," "his gray substance" "receding"
"in the mirror" "I began" "to stare intently" "at my own, &"

"its center changed" "A face" "appeared in it," "a face of mine, but"
"idealized—" "not old, not young—" "though my hair was" "quite dark,"
"with no gray in it" "whatsoever" "But it wasn't" "like young hair,"
"it was like" "the name 'hair':" "a place" "around the face" "Line of

jaw & brow" "& nose" "was" "pure line" "I could have been" "ten or
sixty" "for my skin was not there" "Something like thin paint" "stood
in for it" "But the eyes" "between the lids—" "the lines of lids—"
"were mine," "exactly," "& exactly" "alive" "I stared at" "this

image" "long moments" "till the sticky" "gray substance" "encroached
upon it" "& slowly" "closed over it" "over my face" "Then I left"

"I entered" "a dark cavern" "that had a marked-off" "rear area"
"a little like" "a stage" "but not elevated," "demarcated"
"by four stalactitish boulders" "at the corners" "of its rectangle—"
"The front part" "of the cavern" "was filled with people"

"who blended in" "with its darkness" "so much that" "I couldn't
tell" "if they were dark-skinned" "or just shadowed" "I looked down &
saw" "that my own skin" "now looked dusky" "I felt" "strangely
blissful," "as if my substance," "my flesh," "were permeated" "with

air" "A small transparent" "silver disc appeared" "before my eyes"
"I seemed" "to be seeing" "& hearing" "through it" "Between the
area" "where we were, & the area" "set apart" "was an almost"
"invisible" "veii, perhaps" "of gray air" "And then a man" "walked

through it" "& disappeared" "entirely" "I began to see" "strange
figures" "dim figures" "in that space" "Like moving" "gray line
drawings" "But I couldn't" "make them out, what" "they were, what"
"they were doing" "After a while" "the man emerged" "'I dissolved in

there,'" "he said to us" "'And I seem to" "have had a dream:"
"Instead" "of a body" "I was an object," "a drinking vessel" "of red"
"cut glass" "with figures" "carved around me:" "scenes" "from my
life—" "being a baby," "a boy," "being married," "being old" "I

revolved in space" "being all at once," "all of them, but" "actually"
"being glass" "red glass" "in a world" "of light" "Then someone
filled me" "with water" "& drank from me . . .'" "I laughed at that"
"He said" "to me" "'The water" "was crystalline" "It tasted"

"of herbs" "& river air . . ." "The glass could" "taste the water'"

"I entered" "a cavern" "crowded with" "shadowy people"
"I stood feeling drowsy," "then thought to myself," "'I am now"
"asleep,'" "though I functioned" "as if awake" "Most of"
"the people" "I stood among were men" "I noticed one man" "by his

shirt, a" "dirty red" "Another wore" "a billed hat; &" "many"
"carried bags" "round" "shaped like heads" "There was a
blanket" "spread among them" "of a dirty" "baby blue" "I
knew that" "it was mine," "my bed & house," "my place" "& I

lay down on it" "The floor" "of this cave" "was dirty"
"Brown bugs crawled on it" "A gray-haired woman," "lank-haired
chipmunk-jowled," "speaking to herself, came" "towards me—"
"she smelled of urine—" "hands stretched out, she" "stooped down

towards me" ("her face" "was very mean;" "her hair so shapeless")
"I handed" "her something:" "I discovered" "that it was"
"a sickly" "greenish orchid," "yellow-green" "that looked like
plastic" "As she took it," "as she held it" "I realized"

"it was real" "'I always knew" "it was real,'" "I said—" "was
I lying?" "She vanished" "& I looked up" "at all this"
"crowd of others" "There was a covered" "bowl of food" "at one
corner" "of my blanket" "They stood crowded" "foodless,

blanketless" "I tried" "to will my blanket" "to grow larger"
"'I've been told,' I said," "'that it will grow'" "But I knew I"
"was being false," "& those around me" "were silent" "Then"
"I took the blanket" "picked up my blanket," "stood up &"

"made a shape of it" "a com-" "plicated bundle—" "I acted"
"as if I knew" "what I was doing," "though I didn't" "didn't
really;" "I made it" "into a sort of" "lumpy sphere &" "held it
up for" "all to see" "It was still dirty" "A torn-off satin edge"

"trailed down to" "the floor" "'Will someone take this?' I said"
"A man took it" "& thanked me for it," "not disarranging" "its
shape" "Then I left the cave—" "& woke up," "seemed to wake up"
"as if I had" "been dreaming"

"I entered a cave" "& found a half-mask on the floor" "made of
thin cellophane" "of the sort" "a candywrapper's made of"
"Adhering" "to the cellophane" "were black" "paper shapes,"
"geometrical," "spheres & oblongs" "I put the mask on & said"

"to those in" "the cave—" "they had just entered," "a group of
four or five—" "'We must tear down" "the old structures—"
"the subway" "& other buildings—" "& build beds for" "all the
living'" "'But we have to do" "one hard thing first,'" "a man said,"

"'One thing" "holds us back . . .'" "There was" "too much noise then,"
"everyone spoke" "at once &" "I couldn't hear" "what he said,"
"but knew somehow he was right" "'Someone must do it,' he continued"
"'We will draw cards,' I said," "'for who does it" "The one who

draws" "the highest card" "performs the act'" "The man handed me"
"a deck of cards" "It contained" "the two suits of" "roses"
"& panthers" "Red roses &" "black panthers" "'Which is the
higher suit?'" "someone asked" "'The highest suit" "is a third suit"

"always,' I said," "'& this deck" "contains that suit:" "the
composite suit," "roses/panthers," "half & half'" "Then I myself
"drew the highest card," "the ace of" "roses/panthers" "'I will
do it,' I said" "'You want me, don't you," "to kill the tyrant?"

"I will kill him" "but it won't happen" "quite yet" "I have to
journey first" "farther down" "into this darkness'"

"I entered" "a small cave" "above the door of which" "was written:"
"*A Piece Of*" "*The Tyrant*" "The cave contained" "a table" "over"
"which hovered, like fireflies" "five or six" "constant lights"
"As I came nearer" "I saw that" "there lay on" "the table" "a small

polished stone," "egg-shaped, of lapis," "deep blue" "Whatever
of him it was," "its presence here" "meant, I knew," "that
something of him may be" "indigenous" "to any one of us" "The lights"
"seemed to be guarding it" "I reached for it" "& one" "dipped

suddenly" "& seared my hand" "before I even" "touched the stone"
"The lights now clustered" "close to the stone" "A woman entered"
"the cave" "with a bucket" "full of water" "'They can be" "doused,'
she said" "I took the bucket," "hurled water at them" "Their lights

were quenched, &" "they fell—" "several" "tiny men," "rather
pallid," "green-&-silver winged" "'You mustn't" "harm the angels,'"
"one said in a" "small angry voice" "I laughed & turned to" "the
woman," "'What is this" "blue stone?'" "'A bit of" "the tyrant's

heart,' she said—" "'What do you" "want with it?'" "'I think I'll"
"return it to him'" "I seized it" "from amid" "the little wet-winged
men" "lying helpless" "on the table" "Then I left" "the cave"

"I exited" "from the previous" "cave into" "a corridor"
"which stretched ahead" "as far as" "I could see"
" 'Keep walking,' " "that voice still said to me" "I walked,"
"surmising" "that I was about" "to exit" "this whole system"

"of caves" "The corridor was straight," "the walls & floor"
"quite smooth" "My shoes" "echoed quietly," "I saw no one"
"no one" "I walked for perhaps a mile" "Then I saw" "what I
thought at first" "was a dead end—" "a wall" "As I neared the

wall," "an opening" "in the ground in" "front of it" "became
apparent—" "which turned out to be" "finally" "a staircase"
"descending deeply" "below the level" "of the caves" "I
hesitated briefly—" "the corridor, the" "staircase" "were

so plain &" "so empty" "Then I began to" "descend the staircase"
"I couldn't see" "to the bottom" "of it" "at all" "Somehow the
staircase was lit" "so that only" "those steps were visible"
"that fell directly" "in front of me" "I descended" "& descended,"

"winding round & round," "became" "wobbly-legged," "sometimes
proceeded" "very slowly" "But then" "there was" "a scent in"
"the air" "It was the smell of" "a river," "a smell of water &
weed" "A piece of white down" "drifted past me:" "tule fuzz"

"on a breeze," "a real breeze" "Suddenly I stepped down"
"onto" "earth again" "& passed through a door" "into night air"
"I stood" "on a riverbank," "water flickering" "yellow-white"
"in the electric light" "cast by the bulb at" "this exit" "I wondered"

"if I hadn't" "somehow been here" "before" "A river at night:"
"No," "all rivers at night," "I thought," "are the same—"
"that's all . . ." "Then the voice said," " 'Keep walking' " "I walked to"
"the river's edge," "took off my shoes," "left them there"

"Began to wade" "into the water"

BOOK
three

"The water" "of the river" "was mild-temperatured," "the current
gentle" "I soon began" "to swim—" "in a moonless," "starless darkness"
"The sky held no clouds—" "no luminous" "spheres existed here"
"Yet the sky was" "a sky;" "for the river air" "was fresh & sweet"

"Then," "as I swam," "the others I contained—" "my companions
from the subway—" "weightlessly" "emerged from me," "looking
shadow-like," "& quickly" "solid-bodied" "began to swim with me"
"I never really" "saw their faces" "We swam quietly," "concentrating,"

"our motions almost synchronized" "In the distance sat" "small yellow
lights" "where presumably" "the other shore lay" "Partway across"
"the river," "something else, a substance," "a state of being,"
"a thick noxious" "distress" "in the form of" "a gray cloud,"

"welled up within me" "& left my body" "from a point along" "my spine"
"The cloud" "hovered near us" "& so we turned onto" "our backs to
watch it" "It was full of" "ghoulish faces," "phosphorescent" "death's
heads;" "one skull grew large" "& open-mouthed" "It had long" "glowing

hair," "screamed as if" "in terror," "then spoke" "to me:"
"'We are dying" "You are killing us" "killing us'" "The cloud exploded"
"into greenish flame" "which was soon consumed" "by darkness"
"We turned over" "& resumed" "our swimming"

"Presently" "we neared a pale beach," "narrow" "with trees behind it"
"thick & blue-black," "& lights" "many lights" "deep inside the"
"wooded land" "I touched bottom" "& walked ashore" "Then I saw"
"a final entity," "airy image, pass" "out of my body—" "from my

forehead" "A small shape," "perhaps brain-shaped," "that seemed to"
"contain in miniature" "the cave network" "where I had been"
"I saw the rooms—" "the caverns—" "streaked with color," "dotted with
lights," "but all tiny" "as in a honeycomb" "The image" "receded,"

"gently floated" "away" "on the wind," "like a flower" "a hibiscus—"
"all reds & darks" "& yellow glow—" "Or like a lantern," "paper
lantern" "Then was gone." "The others" "other swimmers" "had not
walked ashore" "with me" "I turned to find them" "I thought they

must be" "still floating" "in the water" "But they had vanished,"
"I was alone" "Myself &" "alone" "Yet emptied" "of much, it seemed"
"I felt unburdened" "& even buoyant"

"I walked into" "the forest;" "for the woods were lit" "by yellow
street lamps" "along various" "dirty pathways" "I paused a moment"
"to absorb" "the texture" "of bark & needles" "The wind carried"
"with a pine scent" "the river's aura—" "delicious air" "Then a

figure" "appeared before me—" "a woman" "in a long dress" "standing
featureless" "in a dark space" "'Welcome,' she said," "& stepped into"
"the light" "She was dark-haired" "but very pale" "I stared hard at her,
realizing" "that her flesh was" "translucent," "& tremulous," "a

whitish gel" "She was protoplasmic-" "looking—" "But rather beautiful,"
"violet-eyed" "'What is this place?'" "I asked her" "'It would be
paradise,' she said," "'but, as you see," "it's very dark," "& always
dark" "You will find that" "those who live here" "are changed"

"enough" "from creation's first intent" "as to be deeply" "upset . . ."
"But you must really" "keep going now'" "'Are those tents" "over there?'
I asked" "I saw small pyramids" "at a distance" "'Yes, these woods are"
"full of beings," "primal beings," "hard to see—" "because it's"

"always dark here" "Most of them" "need not concern you now" "But
wait here," "someone is coming" "to show you your way'" "She stepped
back into" "the shadows," "turned & left me"

"I stood waiting" "for some minutes" "in this very" "alive darkness—"
"the air so vibrant," "the trees awake" "There were flowers," "mixed
grasses," "growing lower" "in the dark," "& I was relieved" "to be
near them" "after so much time" "where nothing grew" "Then" "I heard a

song" "faint & blurred," "a slow song" "I heard it" "as if through
walls" "As if" "there were a room" "next to where I stood" "& someone,"
"a man," "sang inside of it" "The tune was sad," "& attracting"
"I approached it—" "where its source seemed to be—" "& it moved away

from me" "just a" "short distance" "This happened twice" "Then I
understood" "I was to follow it:" "& so it led me—" "through deep
woods" "& clearings," "for" "a long while" "The voice sang" "the
same melody" "over" "& over" "mournful" "& intimate" "in a language"

"I didn't recognize—" "or didn't think I did:" "it was hard to" "hear
the words—" "Till at last we" "reached a meadow" "where the song"
"ceased to sound," "pale & empty" "with trees around it" "Then I
sank to" "the ground" "& fell asleep for" "a long time" "But when I

awoke" "of course" "it was dark"

"I saw, on awakening," "what I had not" "seen before:" "at the
meadow's edge" "etched into the grass" "fine white lines which formed"
"a large curving shape" "I stepped closer" "to see the shape:" "it was
a coiled snake—" "head erect," "tongue extended," "itself thin & long"

"& snakelike," "a snake from" "within a snake's mouth" "I knelt to"
"examine" "the nature of" "the etched lines," "when a powerful"
"gust of wind" "rushed through me" "& stayed blowing" "a gale" "where
I knelt" "It grew stronger" "& more howling" "I fell over" "& thought I

saw" "my head," "my own head," "having been blown" "off my body"
"rolling" "on the grass" "But I also knew" "I was still intact" "Then"
"the wind subsided" "& I saw" "sitting near me," "on a log," "a
headless body," "in a light dress, the" "bloody neck" "black & deep"

"I didn't" "want to look" "but" "of course I had to:" "this headless"
"woman" "was a living personage," "whose hands moved slightly,"
"whose feet shifted" "As I looked at her" "I was filled with" "an oceanic"
"sorrow," "staring at her gruesome neck," "its black well" "I knew she was"

"the one I sought," "our mother," "first woman" "I gripped the earth with"
"my hands" "to stay composed" "And then I heard a voice," "a woman's
voice," "a rich changing voice—" "capable of both" "high & low tones—"
"begin to speak:" "' . . . finally arrived" "You are very" "very late"

"I've been waiting—" "We've been waiting . . . '" "I realized" "that the
voice" "issued from the throat" "of this headless" "body"

" 'I'm late," "am I?' I said" " 'What *time*" is it here," "that I"
"can be late?' " " 'It is,' she said," " 'the long moment" "after my"
"decapitation" "It is a kind of" "forever:" "nearly since" "the world
began" "The holy men," "the wise men," "are frivolous" "& cruel"

"They have invented" "eternities" "but left me here" "for one—"
"They call their visions" "transcendent" "Call me" "accounted for"
"in heaven," "or nirvana," "or wherever," "in extinction—"
"The blessed selflessness" "They were wrong," "I am the same:"

"in time, headless self, &" "suffering" "I have never" "gone to
heaven" "Never died," "never changed" "The truth of us," "the real
truth of us," "is here" "in this darkness," "*is* my decapitation"
"History is eternity" "until this" "is righted—" "No wrong has"

"so long endured" "There can be no truth" "elsewhere," "until"
"this is changed" "The holy men," "the saints," "the wise men," "the
heroes," "the poets" "are ignorant," "are like" "simple drunks' "

" 'I thought" "you would be" "intact here,' I said" " 'I thought"
"there was a place" "where everything was intact" "& this was that place' "
" 'Perhaps you" "are intact somewhere," "but I am not,' she said"
" 'Tell me" "what happened,' " "I said" " 'I'll try,' she said"

" 'In the beginning" "of the world" "there was a whole" "edgeless
entity," "sea of dreaming," "of floating" "changeable shape"
"After a while" "was differ-" "entiation," "as if pieces of sea,"
"of water," "became fish" "As if air" "became birds—" "I can't remember"

"It keeps escaping me" "But the sexes came to be" "in pleasure," "in
glee" "There was much of" "what you'd call" "obscenity" "at the
beginning" "Much orgasmic" "sensation" "permeated" "the primal entity;"
"& when there came to be" "two human sexes," "that was a sharpening,"

"a clarifying" "of the pleasures" "of existing" "The edges" "of our
forms" "made us shiver & gasp—" "This sounds so" "vague, I guess"
"Then something happened" "to the male—" "perhaps because he"
"didn't give birth" "He lost his" "connection" "to the beginning"

"of the world," "to freshness" "of sensation" "To sensation's"
"being soul" "Became a fetishist" "A thinker" "A war-maker" "& ruler"
"Made me dance naked alone" "before all men—" "any man—" "on a
stage, a" "spotlit stage" "Made lewdness" "lose its" "mutuality,"

"its holy aura" "The scales of" "a serpent" "were painted on" "my
body—" "I was stippled" "with diamond shapes" "And as I" "was thus
degraded—" "as all" "went astray—" "I was yet" "the only memory"
"or sign of" "the creation" "I was all there was" "of that" "And so

I endured" "that dance" "I danced" "& I danced" "Nothing" "but sex"
"My head gradually" "over ages" "disattached from" "my body" "as if
by the will" "of everyone" "My body" "still danced then—" "but my
head" "played audience" "to the achievements" "of males" "See it there?' "

"She pointed suddenly" "A head sat" "several feet from us" "with open eyes,"
"frozen eyes," "& fixed" "frozen smile" "Brown skin lifeless," "dark
hair wind-blown" " 'I learned to speak from" "my throat," "from darkness,"
"not from behind the eyes" "Made up stories to tell myself" "through

centuries" "Then one day" "I walked carrying" "my own head" "down through
darkness below the earth," "to this place" "And was forgotten,"
"mostly forgotten," "above the ground' "

"We were silent" "a long moment" "of sadness" "Then I asked her,"
" 'How" "can you see?' " " 'I see,' she said," " 'with my voice," "as I talk"
"I see you" "as we converse" "But I see things" "within myself—"
"pictures, & stories—" "that you might not see" "ordinarily" "I have the

power," "as I speak" "to enable you" "to see them too," "to forget that"
"I'm speaking them" "They take on" "their own life then," "before us,
around us" "I cease to speak" "as they exist;" "though they do" "soon
dissolve," "are never permanent" "For example," "I see this now" "I

see this whole scene:" "A little" "girl's father" "is a corpse in"
"a coffin" "He has swallowed" "a vial of chemicals" "so he will come"
"to life again" "as a ghoul," "a soulless ghoul' " "As the voice spoke"
"I saw before me," "as if in a dream," "the open coffin," "in a house"

"The corpse was handsome," "sapphire-eyed" "Young" "& still alive"
"The vial made him live," "grow facial hair & fangs" "The little girl"
"was very young: five or six" ("The voice still rendered this") "& then"
"slightly older" ("The voice seemed" "to cease now") "She stands"

"in a forest," "looking" "like a girl from" "an antique greeting card,"
"small mouth soft hair," "remote eyes" "conceived by art" "Something"
"she carries" "slowly comes" "into focus:" "a silvery broad axe"
"on a long" "wooden handle," "leaning" "upon her shoulder—" "But the

scene now" "dissolved," "the dream was over" "already" " 'The axe,' "
"said the headless woman," " 'is real now" "& is nearby" "You have brought"
"new power here" "I have never before" "seen an object" "made real
this way" "But the axe" "must become" "a long cloth, I think," "to tie"

"my head back on' " " 'What about" "the ghoul?' I asked" " 'Forget"
"the ghoul for now" "We must tie my" "head back on" "But first" "I will
tell you" "some more of what" "only a throat," "only a headless"
"body knows" "Only your first" "mother knows' "

" 'What" "was it like" "before we first became?' I asked" " 'Can't you
remember" "any more of" "our beginnings—" "that primal entity"
"or how we" "emerged from it?' " " 'How can I" "explain it?" "*Before*"
"life on earth" "I remember" "a surround of" "faces" "in a heaven"

"smiling welcoming" "me" "to exist" "among them—" "Who were they"
"if I" "was to be" "the first woman?" "There is no first, then,"
"only always" "They were the company" "of existence" "Co-angels"
"Co-spirits" "The unborn" "the dead—" "all the same—" "& had I"

"always already" "known them?" "But they were welcoming me" "to this
knowing" "that was existing," "where everything that was to be"
"seemed to exist at once" "Objects" "& events" "in a swirling" "present
moment" "were like bright-colored" "liquid circles," "small light-

streaked galaxies" "Each wheeled" "forever" "& it seemed as if"
"I could know each" "in perfect present pleasure—" "Did I?" "I don't
remember" "For history" "began:" "I was never" "outside of time again:"
"There was the sky now" "& the sea" "A man & I" "stood knee-deep"

"in calm flat sea water" "peering down at" "bright fishes," "red &
orange—" "in flat seaweed—" "& strange sweet" "sea horses" "There was
one of those," "seemingly," "beneath my navel," "deep within me"
"I remember" "no more than that" "of before humans" "became" "I must

honor" "my predicament" "& take you forward" "into history" "Show
you something else' "

" 'My voice" "will show you now,' she said," " 'an early woman,
prehistoric—" "This time" "you will be" "in the story' " "I saw
before me" "a naked woman" "in a tawny plain" "She was brown-skinned,"
"& small," "with tangled hair," "gentle eyes" " 'What happens now?'

I asked" "The woman suddenly" "held a baby" "who fingered" "her hair"
" 'Merge" "with the woman,' " "the voice said to me," "& I walked
towards her" "until we merged &" "I was her" "I held the" "baby closer"
" 'You see,' " "said the voice," " 'you are not" "that much different' "

" 'I can see" "*the phantoms,*' " "I said with" "great certainty"
"For I saw shadowy" "masked figures" "but at a distance" "I felt afraid"
" 'Where are the males?' I asked her" " 'The males &" "their phantoms"
"do something to me," "don't they?' " "The voice said nothing" "Then I

saw the men" "herding the phantoms" "from behind" "with long sticks
& spears" "& I saw that" "the phantoms—" "as the whole horde" "came
closer—" "were like men" "Had ghostly" "human bodies," "but wore dark"
"painted masks" "with geometric" "designs in white lines:" "crude

grimacing" "faces" "Sometimes they walked on all fours" "Sometimes they"
"walked upright" " 'The males,' " "the voice said," " 'periodically"
"are attacked by them" "Sometimes a" "man is killed' " "As she said this"
"I saw the phantoms" "turn back upon" "their herders—" "who quickly

fought them down" "But one was injured," "one man walked now" "with
blood streaming" "from his shoulder" "The men drove the" "phantoms faster"
"Towards me" "Exactly towards me" "I gripped" "the baby hard, but"
"the phantoms" "rushed straight towards us—" "Darkness," "all went

black—" "& when I was" "revived again," "my babe was gone" "The herders"
"had disappeared with him" "I wept with" "grief & rage" "Some men
remained," "tried to comfort me" "with food &" "caresses" "Said, 'Your
child will" "become a man" "He will be taught to" "herd the phantoms' "

" 'But they are phantoms," "only phantoms!' I cried" " 'They can kill now,'
said the men" " 'We have created them" "& they are real" "They can
harm now" "They can harm now" "We can do nothing" "but herd them—"
"Or they" "will turn on us' "

"I became," "perhaps too suddenly," "myself again," "in the meadow,"
"drained & shaken" "as if awakening" "from a nightmare" "My arms
felt painfully" "empty" "of the early" "woman's baby" "'Did I really"
"need to live this?" "Must I know this?' I asked" "'It is" "a true

version,'" "the headless" "woman said" "'A true version" "of what
happened" "long ago" "Though I can't" "remember" "*exactly*" "what happened"
"I" "am only headless," "a headless voice" "Watch my voice now:'"
"Colored lights," "bright pure colors—" "already seemingly" "wordlessly—"

"rose up from" "her throat" "& danced against" "the darkness"
"Turquoise & yellow" "& red spheres," "glowing spheres" "Their dance
relieved my" "grief, somewhat" "There were many" "& they approached me"
"& touched me," "warm" "but not intemperate" "They didn't burn" "my skin"

"The lights cajoled me" "Teased me" "Rubbed my cheek, brushed" "my arm"
"Rested lightly" "on my shoulder" "Then I heard" "the voice say,"
"'. . . The past is shadows" "We'll make" "another child . . .'" "The lights,"
"the lights settled" "in my arms &" "made a shape of" "a glowing baby"

"with a phos-" "phorescent smile" "It was a symbol" "of the future"
"I held it" "Held it" "for a moment" "of peace, till" "it dissolved"

" 'Who" "is the father" "of the baby?' " "I asked her"
"A new stream" "of orange light" "arose from" "her throat"
"& shaped itself into" "a fiery face" "against" "the black night"
"But its outlines" "were sketchy, its character" "unformed:"

"It was simply" "a crude drawing," "large & high," "in front of us"
" 'Where are his sufferings?' I said" "The face" "became more lined then;"
"almost real eyes" "seemed to look at us," "& with interest"
" 'But how is it" "a person," "a man?' " "The face smiled," "became

fleshed with," "successively," "different textures" "of the planet:"
"earth, rock, leaf, water, cloud—" "each was his skin" "a moment"
"And then real flesh," "a human texture" "It seemed miraculous"
"to see flesh on him" "I wanted to" "touch his face" "I felt love for him"

"because" "he had" "my skin" "I loved him for sharing" "my skin"

“But the man’s face” “changed” “It gradually became sad—”
“as I stood there,” “marveling” “at its nuance, its” “expressiveness—”
“The eyes sank,” “their sockets darkening” “Eyes reflecting”
“disappointment,” “pain,” “only the smallest” “spark of life”

“His eyes were light brown” “but bloodshot” “His wide mouth turned
down” “The night” “seemed to get darker” “& creep into” “his face”
“To change from magical” “to deathlike” “Finally” “he spoke:”
“‘We must” “have the child soon—” “must make a” “new future”

“I am dead you know” “I am *dead*” “Years ago I died” “in my suit & tie,”
“in my coffin” “Let me tell you more as we fly . . . ’” “His face diminished to”
“normal size” “He became” “a whole person,” “had a body—” “wore a dark”
“business suit” “He lifted me in his arms” “& flew straight up carrying me”

“We rose high above” “the meadow” “& then drifted” “over the forest”
“black & green” “with the rare shining” “yellow jewels” “that were the
streetlamps” “‘I must,’” “the man continued,” “‘be the father—”
“of this baby that’s not a baby” “Is some sort of” “a future—”

“And as the babe” “is not a babe,” “I will father it” “without
fathering it . . . ’” “‘I think you’re babbling,’ I said” “‘I must,’ he said,”
“‘bequeath my heart” “The love in it was” “pure & true” “many times,”
“many times” “As this flight is pure flight:” “for most intrinsically”

“it is that” “You cannot” “discount my essence” “I must leave something”
“of myself’” “‘Your essence” “has prevailed,’ I said,” “‘for centuries’”
“‘Not my *essence,’* he said” “‘Something in me” “is only pure” “Does not
dominate” “Will not hurt anyone . . . ” “anyone . . . ’” “I realized he was drunk”

“Now we spiraled” “back downward” “‘You must use” “my heart somehow’”
“He handed me” “something pulpy,” “a red organ” “‘You must” “accept
a heart” “I must be part of” “what happens’” “The instant” “we landed”
“in the meadow” “he was gone” “I still” “held his heart” “My hands were

red with” “its blood” “‘What do I do now?” “What do I do with this?’”
“I asked the” “headless woman”

" 'Lay his heart down" "for a moment,' she said," "her voice trembling"
" 'Lay it on" "the grass" "& wipe your hands clean there too—' "
"I did—" " 'Then let's sit" "for a minute" "enjoying this night"
"before we change" "Change forever' " "We sat quietly" "a short while,"

"a mist" "about us now" "that softened" "her headlessness,"
"obscured" "her body slightly," "hid the horror" "of her neck—"
" 'I'm afraid,' " "she said," " 'to take my head back' " " 'Why?' I asked"
" 'I'm afraid" "I'll lose my power" "to speak from" "deep inside of me"

"Lose my power" "to make visions . . . " "But we must put it back on"
"anyway' "
" 'How do we do it?' I asked" " 'Please bring my head here' " "I lifted it—"
"it felt dry," "the face looked chalky" " 'Place it on my neck—"
"I will hold" "very still—" "Now find the heart in" "the grass' "

"I brought" "the heart close" "to the newly" "headed creature"
" 'Smear blood from" "the heart" "on the line of" "separation' "
"I daubed" "a ring of sticky red" "all around" "her neck, like a
necklace" "of liquid ruby" " 'Now find" "the axe," "the girl's axe—"

"Over there somewhere' " "Her voice issued now" "from a pale mouth"
"though the lips" "didn't move yet" "I found" "& brought the axe"
" 'Smear blood on" "the blade's edge,' " "she said" "Which I did"
"The axe went limp" "became a white scarf" " 'Tie the scarf around"

"my wound' " "When I had done so," "her face" "began to change"
"Color" "poured into it:" "her skin was golden brown" "her eyes
deep-set & brown," "tender" "beneath fierce eyebrows" "She was young"
"Younger than I" "& yet she was, I felt," "truly" "our mother . . . "

"Wide nostrils, wide lips . . . " "She smiled at me" "warmly" " 'I'm not
afraid" "anymore,' she said" " 'My voice has not lost" "its power' "

“ ‘My voice has power,’ she repeated” “ ‘More power” “than before”
“For as I’m speaking—” “as I speak now,” “look above us:’ ” “she
pointed” “to the sky, where” “tiny stars” “were coming out”
“just here & there” “in that blackness” “They formed no patterns”

“that I recognized,” “were not at all” “my own stars” “ ‘As I
say a word,’ she said—” “ ‘As - I - say - a - word,’ ” “she said again”
“but in a” “staccato way,” “ ‘a - new - star - appears’ ” “And at”
“each word she said” “a point” “of light appeared” “Meanwhile she”

“touched her own face,” “stroked” “her cheek lightly,” “ran fingers
through” “coarse tousled hair” “ ‘These stars,’ she said,” “ ‘do not
disappear . . .” “They are permanent . . . ” “My voice is making them” “Truly
making them” “As many stars” “as this sky needs” “are as many”

“as I say tonight” “Life is changing” “I have much to do” “And you too”
“have much to do” “You must continue” “your journey’ ” “ ‘Where do I
go now?’ I asked” “ ‘Simply walk towards” “that tall tree,’ she said
pointing” “to a hill in” “the distance,” “just visible” “through a

road’s opening” “in the pines that” “ringed the meadow” “ ‘There is
someone” “waiting there for you’ ” “ ‘But I don’t want to” “leave you yet,’
I said” “ ‘I thought my journey” “might end with you” “I feel that”
“I need you’ ” “ ‘You must take action elsewhere” “& I will be” “with you

really’ ” “Her face glowed” “I awaited” “some sort of” “transmission
from her,” “some sort of” “final miracle,” “final vision” “She merely
handed me” “a small leaf” “ ‘to remember by’ she said—” “& set me”
“on my path” “saying gently,” “ ‘Good-bye’ ”

"I began walking" "towards the hill—" "it seemed to be" "a few miles
away—" "on which small from here," "a sketchy mark," "a tree rose
twistingly," "& disappeared" "into low-lying clouds:" "rose up above"
"the pines, with their intermittent" "lights" "matched now by"

"the new stars . . ." "I walked awhile," "then sat down to rest"
"Fell asleep & dreamed . . . " "The formerly" "headless woman" "materialized"
"as a small form" "from the tiny leaf she'd" "given me" ("it now
rested" "in my pocket") "Materialized" "as a spirit" "with a snake's"

"lower body" "& entered me through my mouth," "down my throat"
"She tasted" "sharp & spicy—" "thymish . . . " "I awoke" "for a moment,"
"then fell helplessly back asleep" "I now dreamed" "I was lifted up"
"& lay floating in air" "amid wings," "many wings" "They were brown"

"& composed of" "softest feathers" "I was in" "a black space"
"with wings & nothing else" "No faced being" "was there" "I felt
comfortable," "protected" "'I am flying,' I thought" "Then I flew through,"
"or I & wings flew," "through" "a sort of barrier" "A blackness"

"ripped open" "like fabric" "or paper . . . " "Then I awoke, but"
"I was no longer" "where I'd fallen asleep" "I was in" "a new clearing,"
"brightly lit" "I saw the tall tree close by," "among pines &
several lamps" "The clearing held" "wooden tables" "with benches—"

"And on one of them," "before me," "perched an owl"

"The owl was brown," "had huge stern eyes," "clear, yellow" "&
staring" "There were countless" "feathers" "on the breast & wings,"
"on its facial disk" "So many," "so many," "that I was" "made dizzy"
"by fixing on them:" "They seemed to ripple" "& multiply" "before my eyes"

"Such a density," "a concentration of" "shifting . . . " "physicality"
"I'd never seen, as on" "this owl's body—" "It *was*" "a small being,"
"though large for" "an owl," "& would be wide-winged, I supposed"
"Away from us, in the trees," "people—" "shadowy people—" "moved

about &" "I saw tents," "green canvas tents there:" "voices blended,"
"laughed a little," "feathered into" "the wind" "I turned back"
"to the owl" "whose gaze had been & was" "on me," "continuously"
"I sensed goodness" "in the creature" "But its sternness" "was forbidding"

"so I waited" "for a sign from it" "Then finally" "our silence broke"
"for the owl spoke—" "though almost" "without moving" "its beak"
"The voice" "seemed to emanate" "from the whole owl—" "a man's voice,"
"measured," "rather gentle," "a lower register of tenor"

" 'Your neck" "is healing,' " "the owl said" " 'My neck?' "
"I touched" "my neck" "& felt a clean thin" "scabbed line"
"all around it" "like a thread—" " 'You have her" "in you now,'
he said" "He turned his whole head" "to the side" "for some moments"

"Then looked back at me" " 'We have" "work to do" "Plans to make' "
" 'What have we" "to do together?' " " 'We must prepare for"
"your confrontation" "with the tyrant' " "He turned his head"
"to the other side" "but continued" "to converse with me" ("From

then on" "he did this constantly" "For he really was" "an owl"
"Always startlingly" "an owl") " 'You have a man's voice,' I said,"
" 'which is familiar" "to me—" "Can you explain this?' " "For
from his voice I" "believed he was" "my father" " 'If I once was"

"a man,' he said," " 'I no longer remember who" "Have forgotten"
"those particulars" "Remember only" "a little" "about being" "a man—"
"Perhaps I knew you?" "Or was your relative?" "That is not relevant"
"to our purpose," "our urgency' " " 'How did you" "become an owl?'

I asked" " 'When I died,' he said," " 'my spirit was released" "& grew
feathers" "one by one:" "an ecstasy" "of finding" "another way"
"of being;" "to become" "another . . . " "material—" "It was so"
"entrapping—" "before I was" "an owl" "Such pain to *think*"

"continually," "of what I'd done" "& would do" "It was too thoughtful
to be a man," "my head full of" "ghosts of acts," "of scenes"
"Full of ghosts of truths—" "do you understand?' " " 'I think so,'
I said" " 'When I" "became an owl" "my feathers" "were what"

"my personality" "became" "Each nuance" "a feather," ("that had been"
"formed in pain") "& I" "became light," "feathery light" "My mind,
my brain," "became these eyes" "I see & hear," "I fly" "I don't
remember" "the past much," "or foresee" "the future" "Excuse me,'

he said abruptly" "He suddenly" "flew up" "on great wide brown wings—"
"Turned to me" "a moment" "in a lovely" "twist of wing" " 'I am
beautiful" "now," "the way a man can't be" ("I will be back"
"shortly' ")

"I waited" "on a bench," "drinking in" "the voices"
"of those I" "couldn't see" "among the trees &" "the tents—"
"Intonations" "of informality," "activity—I" "didn't," "couldn't
make out" "any subjects" "of conversation" "It was simply"

"the music," "the vocal texture" "of beings" "free together"
"I sat enwrapped in—" "unaware" "of how much time passed—"
"The voices murmured, laughed," "shrieked & dropped," "paired &
soloed" "& chorused," "speeded up," "hesitated," "in female,

male &" "childish registers" "All their being" "seemed externalized"
"& hearing them," "mine was too" "Sometimes they seemed to be"
"much closer than" "they were" "Or I myself" "was elsewhere" "than
the bench," "floating" "among them," "bodiless," "lost in voices"

"Bodiless" "in patchy yellow light" "'Perhaps heaven" "is voices,'
I thought," "'speaking voices," "not singing voices" "Perhaps
paradise" "is just like this'" "Someone said" "a slow 'ohhh'"
"Then one of" "the voices" "was an owl's" "hoo hoo hoo hoo"

"For he suddenly" "rejoined me" "Swooped down upon" "the table"
"with a dead" "gray mouse" "in his beak"

"The mouse—" "the mouse's face" "had much beauty" "in its stillness"
"its pink" "front paws" "touched each other, its" "long"
"pink tail" "hung down" "There was" "an air of gravity"
"all about its" "weak body" "The owl" "laid it down"

"on the table" "before me" "& settled" "next to it—"
" 'We shall eat now,' he said" " 'I can't eat a mouse,' I
said" " 'I don't mind" "if you eat it," "but I can't' "
" 'You are" "carnivorous," "try this flesh,' he said,"

"his yellow eyes" "relentlessly" "staring at me"
" 'It is too freshly killed,' I said" " 'My food is killed"
"by others' " "But he only" "kept on staring" "Everything"
"I was saying" "was naked" "& wrong" " 'I don't eat" "my own

prey;" "I mean I" "don't have prey" "Though I eat meat—"
"perhaps I shouldn't" "I shouldn't" "Of course" "all of the world"
"feeds on itself," "doesn't it?" "I mean one form of life"
"or another—" "it's somehow part of" "our unity?" "our union?"

"isn't it?' " "He still stared at me" " 'Of course" "there are
rules" "& I," "I can't kill—" " Oh I'm just babbling' "
" 'Will you eat some?' " " 'Yes,' I whispered" "For I now knew"
"I must" " 'I'll give you" "just a small bit,' " "he said, &"

"with his beak" "he quickly cut off" "a leg & thigh"
" 'Put it in your mouth" "& chew" "for as long as" "you can"
"Swallow" "what you can" "Spit the rest out' " "I thrust it"
"in my mouth" "& began to chew" "before I" "could taste it, its"

"hair & blood," "bone & claw—" "Then it tasted—" "the words
came to me—" " 'like myself," "like myself' " " 'Are you
crying" "for the mouse?' he said" " 'The mouse's" "life"
"takes care of it—" "the life" "takes care of" "the mouse . . . "

"in our case" "that's what happens— ' " " 'I'm crying,' I said,"
" 'because I was" "so hungry' " " 'Do you want more?' " " 'No, it's
enough' " "Then he swallowed" "the rest of" "the mouse whole"
"before my eyes" "& I" "I spat out" "what was left of mine"

" 'It's time to go,' he said" " 'Go where?' " " 'You'll see' " "He
perched on" "my shoulder," "& directed" "me down" "the other side of
the hill" "on top of which" "the camp lay" "I saw a lake below,"
"black & flat," "almost perfectly" "round" "We proceeded to" "a gazebo,"

"an old open" "wooden structure," "with a peaked roof," "at the
water's edge" " 'We will stand here,' he said" " 'What is this lake?'
I asked him" " 'It is the center . . . ' he began" " 'I find it difficult"
"to define" "It is the center" "of the deep . . . " "Of this underworld,

I guess" "But you must" "look into it" "Look into" "the lake' "
"Though the trees" "around the lake" "contained among them many lights,"
"none shone directly" "on the lake:" "it was very" "very black"
" 'How deep is it?' I asked" " 'Infinitely" "deep,' he said" " 'It

connects with" "the great darkness," "connects with" "one's death—' "
" 'Is it—" "can it be—" "really" "water, then?' " " 'Put your hand
in it' " "I did" "& felt nothing" "at all" " 'There is nothing there,'
I said," " 'but it does" "look like water' " " 'Look into it,' the owl

repeated" " 'Don't you see" "something there?' " " 'I see eyes,"
"pairs of eyes . . . " "darkness" "with fishlike" "pairs of eyes' "

"As I stared down" "into the black lake" "I saw more & more"
"pairs of eyes" "The eyes were" "flat yellow" "fish-body shapes,"
"two-dimensional," "with irises suggested by" "drawn-on black lines"
"The eyes were bright," "seemed lit up" "They unpaired," "mixed

together," "swarmed like fish," "yellow fish" "I tried"
"to concentrate" "on the blackness between eyes—" "for hadn't"
"the owl just said" "that the darkness in the lake" "was the great
darkness," "the essence" "of death?" "Wasn't it" "extinction,"

"my own end?" "But the yellow eyes" "multiplied," "became so numerous"
"that the blackness" "was covered over" "by them" "All was eyes,"
"lit eyes," "fish-bodied" "lantern eyes" "'What do you see now?'
said the owl" "& when I" "told him, said," "'Keep trying" "to see

between them'" "And then I" "concentrated" "on a place" "between
eyes," "a thread-thin black line" "As I frowned & stared" "a space
widened" "The expanse of eyes" "was drawn back" "like curtains"
"revealing darkness" "On this darkness I saw" "a person appear"

"composed of more eyes," "composed of tiny eyes," "minute eyes"
"As if the smallest" "constituents" "of matter were" "somehow eyes"
"The person died—" "died then—" "She lay down on black air"
("as if there were" "a bed there") "Air now interspersed," "here &

there, with the" "minute eyes," "to show that air too" "is eyes—"
"Her head rolled" "to the side" "& she was still" "her face partook of"
"the stillness of" "the mouse that" "we'd eaten" "Then she"
"began to decompose" "She decomposed, she changed:" "all of the eyes"

"that had been her" "floated" "away in air" "Her mass of eyes"
"became dispersed eyes," "dispersed everywhere" "'Is there nothing that"
"isn't eyes," "that isn't eyes?' I cried" "'Was she—" "is she only"
"eyes," "all eyes?'"

"The horizontal" "black void" "where the woman" "had lain—"
"defined by dispersed eyes" "as corpse shape" "but empty
black space—" "slowly" "became a play of" "new" "con-
figurations" "Haphazard-" "seeming lines" "of white light"

"began to fill it" "Many lines" "of several thicknesses"
"spread themselves" "throughout the woman's shape," "organizing
themselves" "into an" "apparent system" "like veins" "or nerves—"
"And all the eyes," "all the eyes," "completely" "disappeared"

"All around" "the woman's form" "was even" "blackness now"
"'What does this mean?'" "I asked the owl" "'Who is" "she now?'"
"'She has entered" "the other world," "the simultaneous" "one"
"As when" "you dream" "But it is" "no one's dream" "It is the

other" "being," "free of the body's" "time, its heaviness,"
"the body's slowness compared to mind—" "It is" "as when you
dream," "nowhere" "& everywhere" "She has entered there" "Is
there now" "You must enter" "it too" "before you go back"

"to the tyrant's world" "You must enter that world'" "'How can I
do that?'" "'You will die" "a little death now—'" "He flew
up at me" "Talons thrust at" "my neck" "Pierced me" "And he
pulled me" "into the lake"

"Talons tore me," "tore my flesh," "as I was dragged" "into the
darkness" "The pain was fire in" "spreading pools," "quick-opening
flowers," "fiery blossoms" "with torn" "pecked centers" "Till
all I was was fire" "Fire &" "my screaming" "But soon" "there was

no pain" "There was a numbness" "& an eating" "An eating of" "my
body" "Sometimes" "I was eaten" "Sometimes I watched" "I was
watching" "a woman pecked at by an owl" "Her face was eyeless,"
"pocked with red holes" "Sometimes while I" "was being eaten"

"I was inside" "the owl:" "he would swallow me" "I would float"
"into a warmth," "a dark warmth," "that was his body" "The noise of"
"the eating" "was mutedly" "deafening," "a low crunching" "gulping
noise," "that filled my senses," "myself," "now scattered," "chaotic,"

"dissipated" "into his body," "& also hovering" "outside of it,"
"outside of her" "Then finally" "I coalesced," "was unified" "again"
"somewhere outside in air" "I looked down at her," "my body" "She was
still," "a still lump" "Though strangely" "she was intact now"

"Not eaten," "not even pecked at" "But I was sure she" "was dead"
"I hovered over her quiet face" "tenderly," "recognizing" "this &
that" "idiosyncrasy" "of brow & nose," "of hairline," "of earlobe"
"The owl had vanished," "we were alone" "And then I fell into"

"unconsciousness"

"When I awoke I" "was in darkness" "& could see nothing" "at all"
"I was surrounded" "by voices:" " 'She's come to' " " 'She's ready' "
" 'Please stand up,' one said gently" "I moved" "as if standing up"
"But I seemed to have no form," "seemed to move nothing" "as I made

motions" " 'Very good,' " "the voice said" " 'Have I stood up?' " " 'Yes,'
it said" " 'I can't see anything:" "am I blind?' I asked" " 'There is
nothing here" "to see,' " "one of the voices" "answered" " 'But also"
"you have no senses here—" "you are hearing us" "without ears' "

" 'You don't have" "bodies either?' " "One voice laughed" "a low laugh—"
"I couldn't" "identify" "any voice by sex—" "& said, 'Walk this way' "
"I thought of where" "my legs should be" "& tried to move that," "move
them" " 'Good, good,' " "the voice said" " 'What am I walking on?' I asked"

" 'On nothing,' " "another voice replied" " 'Stop here now" "Someone is
joining us' " "A voice near us," "somewhat more" "authoritative-
sounding," "saying, 'What" "do you wish here?" "You are not really one"
"of the dead' " "The voice was" "before me now" " 'I must,' I said,"

" 'probe being's depth . . . " "Before I try to" "change its surface—"
"But how can I" "not be wholly dead?" "An owl tore me" "apart & ate me' "
" 'That is only" "what you perceived" "The owl is" "very powerful' "
"The voice fell silent" "a moment," "then continued:" " 'Some of your

body parts—" "your *death* body parts—" "parts of your insubstantial
body—" "have been" "replaced" "The owl replaced them" "They will stay
functional" "within your so-called" "real body' " " 'Which parts are
different?' " " 'Your sex is now bone' " " 'My sex?' " " 'Your vagina is

white bone" "& your eyes," "your eyes," "are now like" "an owl's eyes"
"Though they seem more like" "two black flowers—" "two black hollyhock"
"flowers" "They are black flowery" "craters" "You are now equipped"
"to experience" "what you need' "

" 'We will be silent" "& wait,' " "the voice said" "Then we were
truly quiet" "& being that," "were nothing" "Really nothing" "but
the darkness" "This moment was very long," "Very long &" "very wide"
"It had a" "vast diameter" "I felt as if" "I could be" "falling

asleep forever" "Then I saw it" "coming towards me—" "so stately,"
"so stately—" "a light," "a white light" "A radiant" "small sphere,
I guessed" "Diameter" "of but a few feet" "It was seeking" "me out,"
"this light so" "unexpected" " 'What is this light I see?' " "I asked the

voices" " 'You are blind,' " "the voices whispered" " 'You are blind' "
" 'You do not *see* it' " " 'You have no senses' " " 'You are effectively"
"dead' " " 'I see it,' I said" " 'It is a small light—" "It lights up
nothing" "There is obviously" "nothing here" "But it is beautiful"

"Beautiful' " " 'It is not a light,' " "the voices said" " 'It is yourself' "
" 'It is something like" "yourself' " "Then the authoritative" "voice said,"
" 'We are going to" "leave you now' "

"I looked into the light" "directly" "with what I knew to be black eyes"
"Light streamed down through" "my eyes" "into myself" "And"
"as if inside me" "were only mirrors" "which faced each other" "I
felt myself" "light up within," "entirely," "the length of me"

"I was sight," "pure sight" "Was being," "was seeing," "with no object"
"whatsoever" "Nothing to see," "nothing to be:" "There was" "an other
though—" "the light which lit me" "& I loved it" "most purely"
"though I" "was also it" "'Is this" "the deepest darkness?'" "I

asked it" "'It is,'" "it said," "in no voice at all" "'It's what you've
always" "suspected" "It's nothing but" "what you've always known,"
"always been" "For you've always" "been being" "It's simple" "Simple'"
"'This light,' I said," "'our light," "is the same as the" "surrounding

darkness'" "'Of course,'" "said the light" "'Both" "are being"
"There is no darkness" "or light, here" "But when I leave you" "you
will be lit—" "even if the light" "does diminish'" "We were silent"
"awhile;" "then I spoke again:" "'I'm at peace with" "being" "In

this moment" "I've become" "all that" "I am" "I'm ready" "to
go back'"

"Slowly" "the sphere receded" "& disappeared" "into darkness,"
"retreated backwards" "to a pinpoint" "& vanished—"
"My light shone brightly" "for some time," "then its intensity"
"diminished" "to a moonlight-like" "pearlescence," "a consistent"

"soft glow" "Then I saw" "that nearby" "was a skeleton," "my
skeleton," "sent close to me" "by whatever" "agency" "of this
so-called lake—" "My face was gone" "My flesh was gone"
"I recognized" "my own bones" "only" "by instinct" "I wondered"

"what the purpose" "of my body" "had been:" "I felt" "affection
for it" "but its individualities," "recollected," "seemed
small & tame," "its capabilities so mild," "its sorrows" "too intense"
"I sat beside" "my skeleton" "I knew that" "I had to" "somehow"

"reinhabit it," "reinhabit it & return" "It lay" "on its back:"
"so I stretched out" "on top of it—" "on my back—" "& slowly"
"sank down within," "sank down & stretched around" "I inhabited it"
"somewhat now," "almost being" "my own bones" "My bones" "were full

of knowledge," "the history" "of the planet" "As I put them on"
"I saw shapes" "in the darkness" "before my eyes—" "dreamy figures
& scenes" "I saw amoebas" "swell & divide" "Saw apes die" "& be mourned"
"I saw a king" "in blood-soaked velvet" "standing" "in a puddle,"

"a small puddle" "of blood" "The blood smelled" "like rotted orchids"
"All the trapped light" "of creatures" "seemed so dirty" "& scuffed,"
"so neutralized," "debilitated" "So obscured"

"I felt skin" "begin to grow on me," "grow on me" "again" "Felt
organs, within," "swell & flower, blood flow" "The I" "that had
just been—" "that had been light," "pure light—" "now shivered"
"with pleasure" "to be entrapped" "by flesh" "My senses" "were

delectable;" "my mouth gasped" "at its own moistness" "But the
tyrant's" "body," "dream-image of it," "now appeared" "floating
stretched-out" "above me," "face down," "face near mine—"
"dressed in his dark suit & tie" "As if" "to enter me too,"

"mingle with" "my flesh & organs" "Dwell within me until I died"
"I caught his large blue smiling eye" "His right eye swelled"
"& enlarged" "Enlarged, disattached" "& came closer" "It was
full of type," "of letters," "slightly raised &" "in a spiral"

"All the excess light" "that hovered" "about the outside" "of my
body—" "that had not been" "enclosed by it—" "was sucked up into"
"those letters," "till the letters" "glowed white" "His eye"
"was replaced" "within his face" "His smile grew larger" "'It all"

"becomes yours" "Becomes yours,' I whispered" "The tyrant's"
"image vanished" "by sinking down into me" "Yet I felt my"
"flowered owl eyes," "my bone vagina," "in place beneath" "my flesh"
"& I heard" "a voice whisper—" "the authoritative" "voice—"

"'Do you feel" "a tightness" "about your mouth & nose?'" "'Yes,"
"underneath,' I said" "'Underneath as if" "within the bone'" "'You
have grown" "a hidden beak,' it said," "'an owl's beak—" "Don't
forget" "that you have it" "for you will use it'"

"I must have slept then," "long & deeply" "Hours passed," "perhaps days" "I dreamed" "at one point," "as I had" "once before," "that I was carried in flight" "through the darkness" "among wings" "When I awoke" "the owl's face" "was above me" "And I" "was at the

campground" "in the forest" "'You brought me back" "from the lake,' I said" "'Do I really" "have a beak?'" "The owl nodded" "He pressed liquid" "to my lips" "brushed my face with" "his wing"

"The owl" "held a wooden cup" "of broth to" "my lips—"
"it smelled of mice," "smelled of warm fur" "& meek blood"
"People stood round," "human figures," "bending over me in a blur"
"The owl motioned" "them away" "with his long soft brown wing"

"Brown, dark" "& light" "Scalloped" "with finger shapes"
"It was beautiful—" "his wing—" "as I awakened," "alive" "in the
forest" "'I think" "you can sit up,' he said," "I slowly pulled"
"myself up" "He perched next to me" "'You are ready,' he said"

"'Ready" "for the tyrant—" "except for one thing—'" "He drew his
left claw to his beak" "& in an instant" "extracted a"
"long talon" "His claw bled" "'Give me your right hand'" "I
extended it" "He cut it quickly," "painlessly" "an incision"

"on the back of it—" "with his right" "middle talon" "& then
inside the" "incision" "he inserted" "the extracted one"
"'You now have" "a talon," "your own talon,' he said" "'You have
weapons—" "& your travail—" "with which to face him" "Your

weapons" "are moral" "They were given you" "by an animal"
"Manufactured" "by nature," "were made by nature" "Not by"
"the human mind" "Not a rational" "device," "not a vicious" "device"
"You are now part owl'" "He flew up" "& hovered" "before my face"

"Extended" "his bleeding claw" "& smeared" "a drop of blood"
"on my forehead" "'When the time comes," "think like me,' he said"
"'Not like" "a human woman" "but like an owl'"

" 'How will I return" "to the tyrant's world?' I asked" " 'That tall
tree,' the owl said," " 'leads upwards" "to a doorway" "beneath"
"the tyrant's house" "I will now take you there myself' " "Then people
came" "& crowded round me" "They were human" "yet ethereal" "They were

like motion" "of humans" "For they were always" "moving, talking,"
"laughing" "or singing" "Were busy" "& also airy" "& when someone, say,
moved her arm," "an afterimage" "of that motion" "lingered" "in the
air" "One of them—" "a man," "with a face both" "old & youthful,"

"said, 'Don't let" "the tyrant fool you" "He can fool you into"
"despair &" "submission' " "Then a woman" "tied a cloth," "a clear
red sash," "around my waist" "Kissed me lightly" "on the cheek
"The owl said," " 'It's time to go' "

"The owl" "led me, flying," "towards the thick black tall tree"
"It was obscure," "swathed in mist" "Had no visible" "leaves or branches"
"It was a long naked tree trunk" "as far as" "I could tell"
"'You have something,' said the owl," "'that belongs to" "the tyrant,"

"something" "in your pocket'" "I remembered" "I had a piece of"
"the tyrant's blue lapis heart" "My hand" "closed around it" "'You will
use it" "when you arrive" "to draw the tyrant" "to the door—"
"He must unlock it" "& admit you" "And now" "we will fly upwards"

"I'll be your wings" "My wings behind you" "will elevate" "& guide you"
"But in the tyrant's world," "you must fly alone'" "'I will fly?'
I asked" "'You are owl,' he said," "& then darted" "behind me"
"'Lift your arms out," "straight out" "from your sides'" "He spread

his wings out" "behind my outstretched arms" "& we began to" "ascend"
"Rode the air up" "I rode the air" "through much mist" "& darkness"
"The new stars glinted sometimes" "through foggy patches" "like mica pieces"
"Soon we entered" "an opaque darkness" "& the air became" "stale & close"

"'We are in a" "vertical tunnel" "piercing the caves &" "subway system"
"It encloses" "the tree" "The tree's few branches—" "at its very top—"
"are embedded in" "the foundation" "of the tyrant's house—'"
"Presently" "he said, 'There it is," "the tyrant's basement" "& there's

an opening" "the years have made," "that ages" "have made'" "It was
a small" "jagged black hole—" "we were illuminated" "murkily"
"by an electric bulb" "somewhere above" "'Squeeze on through it now,'
he said" "'. . . through the hole—" "climb up—" "there!'" "I knelt on"

"the floor" "peering down at" "the owl" "'A stupid place,' I said,"
"'for good-byes'" "'I have only" "one expression" "for my face,' he said"
"'I can't smile" "I can't cry" "I have my owl look—" "'Good-bye, my dear'"
"Immediately" "he began" "to descend"

BOOK
four

"I stood before" "a dismal door," "an old paint-eroded" "wooden door"
"I took from" "my pocket" "the fragment of" "the tyrant's heart"
"& held it," "just held it," "standing there in" "murky brown light"
"The lapis" "now had" "a pulse in it:" "one place throbbed rhythmically,"

"as if the stone were," "really, blue flesh" "The lapis soon" "became
luminous," "haloed" "Proximity" "to its owner" "was making it
come alive—" "& I felt it" "exert" "a pull outwards" "into the
building" "It grew heavier" "& more vibrant," "as I stood there,"

"reflecting" "on my recent" "ordeal," "my death into" "the lake"
"I felt joyous" "but knew" "that I must subdue" "my joy" "I searched
my depths for" "another character," "a self appropriate" "to what I
must do—" "to what I must do now" "My face changed—" "I felt the change—"

"into a former" "mask of sorrow" "Lines deepened in" "my cheeks,"
"deepened near" "my eyes" "Then I heard footsteps beyond the door—"
"heard the lock turn" "Abruptly" "the tyrant" "stood before me"
"Gray-haired, blue-eyed" "Very tall" "Charged up" "with anger" "He said,"

" 'You are presumptuous" "Only" "presumptuous" "That is all that"
"you are" "There must be little else" "in your soul . . .' " "He snatched
the lapis" "from my hand," "then said sarcastically," " 'Won't you"
"come in?' "

"I didn't move" "at all," "stared at the tyrant," "at first seeing"
"only a" "remembered face," "recalled from" "screens & pictures"
"White-haired" "round-eyed image," "thin lined cheeks—" "his
photograph" "Then in the glare of" "his intensity" "for a moment"

"I thought" "I might perversely" "become drowsy" "become sluggish"
"or still . . . " "The moment lengthened . . . " " 'Come this way *please!*' "
"The tyrant grabbed me" "by an elbow," "led me" "down a hallway,"
"up a staircase—" "I stole sideways" "looks at him—" "boyish,

lanky" "in his dark suit" "But was there something" "slightly in-"
"substantial" "about his being?" "It seemed to me" "that his body"
"was . . . " "not all there" "His limbs looked" "slightly airy,"
"slightly marbled" "with air," "slightly streaked" "with absences"

"Small, very small" "pieces of" "his face," "patches" "of his hands"
"weren't there" "And yet he had" "all force & presence" "His grip on"
"my elbow" "was very" "very strong &" "his opaque" "blue eyes"
"were whole" "& disconcerting" "He led me into" "an immense" "tiered

room—" "museum hall—" "with a central" "open space," "& many levels"
"of balconies" "lining" "the walls" "On each level" "were cases"
"full of animal" "& plant specimens," "full of artifacts" "& dioramas"
"The whole was lit by" "a domed skylight" "But the light from it"

"was not bright, &" "suspended" "near the ceiling," "partly blocking"
"the light," "causing shadows everywhere," "was a large" "plaster brain,"
"apparent model" "of a brain" "The tyrant led me" "to the court"
"in the middle of" "the ground floor" " 'So,' he said," " 'so,"

"Miss Owlfeathers," "you're here without" "appointment" "returning
a piece" "of my heart" "to me' " "He tossed it up" "& caught it"
"Then he grinned—" "his mouth was very wide" "He looked" "almost zany—"
"He dropped the stone in" "his jacket pocket"

" 'You are casual" "with your heart,' I said" " 'This piece,' he said,"
" 'is all that's left of" "my personal" "heart" "It belongs in"
"the caves" "as a reassuring" "symbol' " " 'Have you no real heart?'
I asked" " 'A heart" "has grown to be,' he said," " 'superfluous" "to me"

"inasmuch as" "I have become" "reality, itself" "I am reality,
itself" "My 'heart' is" "probably everywhere . . ." "anywhere . . .' "
"I felt that" "he was lying" "& didn't know why" "he might be doing so"
" 'In the subway,' I said," " 'is it there?" "Is your heart there?' "

" 'The subway" "is surely" "the same as" "my heart,' " "he said with"
"sudden intensity" " 'Then:" " 'I understand you've" "come to kill me' "
"His large blue eyes," "round blue eyes," "unblinking," "fixed on me"
" 'So kill me," "so kill me,' " "he said" "I was" "disconcerted" "I had"

"at that instant" "neither impulse" "nor ability—" "felt no directive"
"whatsoever—" "to kill" "this person" "standing next to me"
"I wanted merely" "to be there," "like myself in" "most moments,"
"fairly comfortable," "& not taking" "drastic action . . ." " 'We'll see,' "

"I said" " 'But I'm not vulnerable," "not vulnerable" "at all,' "
"he said" " 'I'm not even" "a real person' " " 'Not" "a real person?' "
" 'Why else" "do you think" "bits of my body" "are airy," "seem to be
missing?" "You didn't" "really think" "you could kill me," "just

kill me?" "Kill me & change the world?' " "He laughed" "& laughed some more"
"I half believed him," "half didn't" " 'Come tour" "my house with me,'
he said" " 'You can't kill me;" "so join me" "for now' "

"We walked past displays" "of dead animals" "behind glass" "Climbed
from balcony" "to balcony" "in the erratic" "weak light" "It was the
first" "natural light" "I'd seen in years—" "it seemed nothing,"
"meant nothing" "I had a grievous" "impression" "of a hallful" "of eyes:"

"monkeys' eyes," "fishes' eyes" "Eyes of tigers" "& rhinos" "Eyes of
falcons," "of ospreys" "The eyes, even" "of owls:" "a case of owls,"
"all dead-alive" "& affecting" "Were owls' eyes" "not my own eyes?"
"or the eyes of" "my own—" "my own," "my owl?" "It was the same look."

"the one owl look," "as when he'd" "said good-bye" "But I also" "saw
human eyes:" "there were" "dioramas" "of groups of humans—" "models,
not real—" "but with lifelike" "glassine eyes," "lucid," "lucid as"
"the outer domes of" "cats' eyes" "The humans" "were in ethnic"

"& historical" "environments" "In various robes," "veils & turbans"
"In tents or houses" "of lacquer, bamboo," "hides or wood" "But one"
"diorama" "was of a subway car," "in darkness," "as if in motion"
"Through the windows" "one saw stiff figures" "standing," "holding poles"

"Or sitting" "on metal benches . . ." "Still, they were" "so still"
"with those grave" "glassine eyes" "And on one bench" "head framed—"
"head framed by" "a window—" "sat . . ." "it was myself," "an exact figure"
"of myself," "unsmiling," "somber, shadowed—" "mentally shadowed"

"I winced" "& glanced up" "Looked up at" "the tyrant" "He smiled"
"a small smile," "the smile of" "the self-pleased" "Then directed"
"my attention," "with a motion" "of head & hand," "toward another"
"diorama:" "a bedouin-" "like woman" "who sat weaving" "a basket"

"Draped in" "rich black robes" "Weaving" "a tan basket" "with a single"
"red stripe" "I was sure" "she was the woman—" "the one from" "the caves—"
"who had woven" "me," "who had called herself" "my history" "She was
as still as" "all else here—" "'How did you know?'" "I whispered"

"'I told you" "I told you" "I am reality,' he said" "'No you aren't,'"
"I said fiercely," "but I wasn't sure" "'Were you with me" "when I died?"
"When I died into" "the dark lake?'" "'Yes,' he said," "'yes, I was'"
"in a slightly stiff," "slightly false" "intonation" "He was lying"

" 'Would you like to see" "my government?' " "he said, obviously"
"to change the subject" "He led me" "toward miniature" "dioramas,"
"scenes that sat on" "waist-high pillars—" "involving" "tiny figures"
"an inch," "two inches high" "Some showed" "men in suits & ties"

"in conference" "around tables" "One showed" "a large assembly of
such men," "most seated," "one standing" "as if orating," "one
presiding" "at a desk" "The figures" "had painted faces" "& were
each alike" "The rooms themselves," "the little rooms," "were built of

rich brown wood pieces" "with deep green & red" "rugs & curtains"
"Exquisite small-paned" "louvered windows" "minute golden" "light
fixtures" "As I looked at" "the legislature," "the body" "of men in
session," "I saw that" "the orator's mouth" "seemed to move"

"His hand moved too," "up & down" "in a short" "repetitive gesture"
" 'Clockwork?' I asked" " 'This *is*" "my legislature," "real legislature,'
he replied" "He lifted" "the glass" "that enclosed this petite scene"
"& I heard" "a soft squeaking sound" "continuous" "& undulant"

" 'That is his voice,' he said" "He replaced the transparent hood"
" 'I keep telling you," "I keep telling you:" "all" "exists in me' "

"The tyrant" "next led me" "away from the" "tiered balconies"
"through a door" "& into" "a high-ceilinged" "darkened hall—"
"full of visages," "full of masks—" "a room of faces" "with holes
in them" "Eye- nose- & mouth-holes" "'What are these masks of?' I asked"

"'Oh I suppose . . . " "Well *these* are" "masks of principles," "essences"
"For example," "this is a mask of" "vegetation'" "It had a grain-"
"of-wood face," "with leaves for hair" "'This one's a mask,' he said,"
"'of cities'" "It was painted" "to look composed of" "red bricks with"

"white mortar" "'Mask of . . . sexuality!'" "He laughed at it" "It had a
penis nose," "vagina mouth," "nipple eyes" "'Mask of childishness!'"
"A bifurcated" "baby's face," "one-half laughing," "one-half bawling"
"'These masks" "are not all" "of the same type,' I said" "'What

are those" "demonic faces?'" "For the far wall" "was hung with crudely"
"caricatured" "expressions of" "ferocity" "& viciousness," "unclear,
shadowed" "from where I stood" "'Those are—'" "we approached them—"
"'the literal faces," "real faces," "of warriors," "conquerors . . .'"

"I could see now" "that they were that—" "beneath thick red &" "black
lines" "were stretched dead faces," "real skin" "Coarse brown-discolored"
"dead-hide skin," "eyes shut," "sewn shut" "Mouths sewn shut" "The
grotesque" "caricatures" "were an overlay" "in lipstick" "& greasepaint"

"'These also" "exist in you?' I asked" "'There have always been"
"such men,' he said" "'They must be natural . . . " "inevitable" "But come see"
"some other masks'" "He took me" "to one more display:" "Masks of Jesus,"
"of Buddha" "Jehovah-like" "faces" "Masks of nameless" "tribal deities"

"Masks of gods" "from everywhere" "He placed a golden" "Buddha-mask"
"on his face" "'Why would you want to" "kill such as this?'" "he said
playfully" "'Such a mildness" "as this?" "Am I not this too?" "Or,"
"for that matter," "am I not you too?" "What would be" "left of you?"

"If you killed me?'"

" 'Now step behind" "this display case,' he said" "The case itself—"
"it sat some feet from" "the wall—" "was full of" "feather fetishes . . ."
"bark placards . . . " "sticky-looking" "lumpy spheres" "of whatever"
"dark secretions" " 'You own their magic too . . . ?' I began" "And then saw"

"on that wall" "a large" "lone mask" "of the woman" "who had been
headless," "our first mother" "The mask of her" "was lifelike;"
"flesh of painted wood" "well-colored" "Its warm brown," "smooth brown,"
"picked up green &" "violet highlights," "skimming," "elusive"

"The hair was spread out around her head—" "tangled" "coarse real hair—"
"as if she were" "a pinned sun" "And there were no eyes—" "black
holes," "empty sockets" "Though her wide nose," "her flat pretty nose,"
"was well-rendered" "Her lips were parted" "revealing blackness"

"But were parted" "in ambiguity" "of expression—" "about to speak?"
"At the threshold" "of some unpleasantness?" " 'Yes, it's she,' "
"the tyrant said" " 'It is her mask" "her head' "

“ ‘She left us long ago” “Found it intolerable” “to have become”
“a symbol,” “empty symbol’ ” “ ‘You destroyed her,’ I said” “ ‘Enslaved
her” “& destroyed her” “She expected—” “at least at first—”
“power & influence” “equal to” “any man’s’ ” “His eyes tried”

“to hold me still,” “hold me” “& impress me” “ ‘Soulfulness,’ ” “he
continued,” “ ‘cannot hold power” “or hold its own” “What she had could not”
“hold its own—” “wit & warmth” “& beauty” “are weak &” “exploitable,”
“vulnerable” “to our enemies—’ ” “ ‘Our enemies?’ I asked” “ ‘Don’t you”

“contain them too?’ ” “He ignored me” “& said,” “ ‘Such qualities”
“are contrary to” “Nature’s scheme for” “who holds sovereignty’ ”
“ ‘You are, I take it,” “Nature,” “contain Nature?’ ” “I said mockingly”
“He modestly inclined his head” “ ‘As the scientist I am—” “witness my

house—” “I do,’ he said” “ ‘From the outside, I admit, but” “I do”
“rule Nature” “Understand” “& rule it” “& have increasingly” “since she
left us” “for the darkness . . . ’ ” “He regarded” “her mask now” “ ‘After”
“she left,” “we began” “to forget” “exactly who she was” “Though we

remembered” “the feeling of her” “We invented” “songs about her . . . ’ ”
“The tyrant quietly” “began to sing:” “ ‘When the snake” “was our mother,”
“when the snake” “was the train . . . ’ ” “Sang several” “of the old verses”
“but added ones” “new to me:” “ ‘We serve her memory now” “in pain”

“We serve her memory now” “in pain” “When” “we ride the subway,”
“we ride inside” “her memory;” “when” “we ride the subway,” “her metal
ghost,” “her worthless ghost” “For she was generous,” “she was sinuous”
“And when we ride it,” “when we ride it,” “aren’t we lifeless?” “Aren’t we

worthless?” “Aren’t we metal” “but for our pain?” “Except for” “our pain?’ ”

"The tyrant's" "song was over" "He stood staring" "marble-eyed"
"at her brown" "distressed mask-face," "brown" "sunburst head"
"I myself" "felt my own face" "harden further" "into its sorrow mask"
"'Let's move on,' he said" "He took me" "through a back door" "to a

stairwell—" "where there was" "a small window" "with half-"
"open slats;" "the light that fell through" "the slats" "was muted,
grayed," "almost twilit" "I paused" "at the window" "'Why is your house"
"so shadowy?" "And why is" "the light so dim?' I asked" "'Because,'

he said," "'we're in my body . . . " "It's all inside me" "quite literally"
"And outside" "this building" "is inside me too . . . " "My thoughts are"
"half-material" "& make a screen in" "the sky" "above the world'"
"I looked out between" "the slats" "I saw clean white" "apartment buildings;"

"& trim avenues" "adorned with" "beds of red but" "pale tulips—"
"a tomato-cream" "color—" "interspersed" "with grape hyacinths"
"whose purple was" "mostly gray" "There were trees," "young trees,"
"groomed &" "unfertile" "Well-to-do-" "looking people" "walked briskly,"

"hailed pale cabs" "They looked very like—" "from where we stood—"
"the people" "in the small" "dioramas," "as if their features"
"had been painted on" "by a tiny" "fine-haired brush:" "explicit eyebrows,"
"nostrils, mouth-line" "All & only" "in place"

"The sky, the far air" "had a grainy," "a patterned" "gray look,"
"as if there were a" "thin lace curtain" "hung in front of it"

" 'There are other wings" "to my house,' " "the tyrant then said" " 'I can show you" "libraries," "art galleries," "& gardens—" "gardens full of" "statuary" "I can show you" "old manuscripts . . . " "icons . . . " "codices . . . " "Scrolls & tablets . . . " "Or greenhouses," "if you like:"

"I have orchids" "& begonias . . . " "Also herb gardens," "wild flowers' " "Suddenly" "I heard a rumbling," "a rumbling noise" " 'The subway," "is it the subway?' I asked" " 'Of course,' the tyrant answered" " 'Can you take me there?' I said" " 'Is that really" "where you'd like to go?' "

" 'I haven't been home" "in a long while,' " "I said carefully," "wondering" "where my home was," "where my home now was" ("Where my true home" "Where my true home . . . ") "In that great" "unhappy subway world" "some calling" "homelike element—" "something" "black &

ragged" "like a lost piece" "of soul—" "seemed to" "reside" "Something" "that needed tending to" " 'I haven't been there" "in a while" "myself,' " "he said," " ' . . . remiss in" "my duty' " "We began to" "descend the stairs" "Then at one landing" "he said, 'Wait here' "

"He slipped through" "the door there" "Soon came back in" "an old suit," "navy-blue" "with shiny" "& slightly" "frayed edges" " 'I'm in disguise,' he grinned" "He was now" "brisk & light" "At the bottom of" "the stairwell" "he took a key from" "his pocket" "& unlocked" "the steel door"

"When the lock turned" "he winced slightly," "his hand flew" "to his chest—" "some passing pain" "Then we entered" "a darkness full of" "a familiar" "roaring sound" "Engulfed again," "engulfed again in" "that sound"

"As" "my eyes adjusted" "I found that" "the darkness" "was actually
dimly lit by" "naked low-wattage bulbs" "We stood" "on a ramp,"
"the other side of" "the door," "that was meant to" "bridge a stretch"
"of abandoned" "subway track" "The ramp was broken" "in the middle;"

"could not be used" "The tracks were covered" "with rats—" "open-"
"mouthed rats" "Their heads & mouths" "turned up towards us"
"Everywhere I
looked" "below us" "were only" "open rats' mouths," "mouths with
bared teeth" "'The subway" "has become" "more extreme" "since you left it"

"More strange &" "dangerous," "more violent,'" "the tyrant said to me"
"'How can we enter here?' I asked" "The tyrant, who was" "excessively
long-legged," "like a dancer," "a ballet dancer," "leaped across"
"above the rats' mouths," "his legs split straight out" "Then stood on"

"the other side" "'Leap across,' he said" "I stood frozen" "I was no
athlete" "'Isn't," "isn't this" "your *home?*'" "he taunted" "Enraged I
leaped out" "& fell downward," "towards the rats" "Then time slowed"
"Slowed" "For in" "the split-second" "in which I was" "in air"

"I heard" "the word 'SAVED'" "spoken three times" "by an unknown voice"
"Then I hovered" "above" "the open rats' mouths—" "perhaps I"
"lost consciousness?" "lost consciousness" "just a second" "Then"
"I was beside him," "stood beside him on concrete" "with no sense"

"of having actively" "crossed the space" "'I don't know how" "I came across,'
I said" "'It felt as if" "I were dreamed across," "another self in me
spoke" "& then dreamed me" "across . . .'" "'You became an owl,'"
"the tyrant said" "'For an instant," "a brief instant," "you looked like"

"an owl's shadow" "& you flew" "You flew across'"

"Then we passed through" "another door" "& onto" "an ashen platform"
"I was back now," "the air unmoving," "the stained walls sallow"
"Bodies of sleeping men" "in colorless" "dirty blankets like" "grimy
pale flesh" "lay" "at my feet" "A woman" "was begging," "was begging"

"with a cup" "She wore a ragged blouse" "that was map," "that was
printed as" "a red-lined map" "'What map is" "on your blouse?' I asked"
"'Map of" "Map of" "Map of the subway,' she said" "'But it looks,' I said,"
"'so arterial—" "the lines so red & thick'" "They seemed to thicken"

"as I looked at them" "One line upon her chest" "swelled especially,"
"as she" "began to speak:" "'He said we were" "his lifeblood" "He
said we were" "his heart" "Am I inside" "someone else's," "someone"
"else's self?" "How can I live?" "How can I live my life?" "It's all"

"too close in here . . . " "Living" "someone else's . . . " "Dying close . . . "
"You're all too close . . . '" "She wandered off" "babbling lowly" "to
herself" "I looked at" "the tyrant's face," "shadowed," "unsmiling"
"'You look frightened,' I said" "'May I confide" "in my would-be"

"assassin?' he asked" "'The darkness—" "this darkness—" "scares me,"
"always scares me" "Rises up" "inside me" "like a disorienting"
"substance," "something" "close to deadly . . . '" "'Why have you not"
"tried to change it?" "Tried to change this dark place?'" "'Because"

"it is inside me" "It is" "my heart" "My lifeblood, my heart" "It is
my real heart:" "how could I change that?" "This being has this heart"
"Of course, my dear," "it is not flesh—" "I am not vulnerable—"
"But being this way" "for thousands" "of years," "I cannot change"

"It cannot change'" "As he spoke, I" "became more certain" "he was
vulnerable somewhere" "Perhaps somewhere not far" "I did not speak this
thought" "Instead I said," "'You consider" "your heart" "to be dis-
ordered?" "In a state of" "disorder?'" "'It is chaotic," "desperate"

"So full of feeling," "it is intolerable . . . " "It is also" "my courage'"
"He gave me a" "fierce look," "a sudden hard" "all-alive look"
"'And that is why" "you won't kill me" "All these feelings" "are
empowering" "Their intensity" "gives me power" "Look" "a train is coming"

"Let's get on it,' he said"

"The car we entered" "contained a crowd" "of people" "around one bench,"
"around one bench only" "We pressed through them" "to the front"
"'He is dying,' a woman said" "The man lay outstretched on the bench,"
"his space" "demarcated" "by a rectangle of" "small red lightbulbs—"

"lay" "on his back—" "a dark man" "with a dusty face," "emaciated,"
"in torn clothes—" "cheeks sunken, lips drawn" "Eyes protruding,"
"eyes huge" "'He is going now,' a voice said" "And he had died—" "he had
died, though" "his eyes" "did not close," "but his face" "became still,"

"its color fell" "a shade grayer" "& all" "electric force," "all
spirit was gone" "A brown" "rough blanket" "was drawn up over him"
"The tyrant" "began to weep" "'Are your tears" "precious jewels"
"as they say?' I said angrily" "For a woman knelt" "near the dead man"

"weeping red tears," "weeping blood" "'I cannot,'" "said the tyrant,"
"'be held" "responsible . . .'" "His sentence" "was interrupted"
"A man had shoved through," "pushed us aside" "& stood near" "the victim"
"He was trying" "to speak," "but his lips seemed sealed shut;" "protruding"

"were sealed shut" "Then" "the words finally" "forced" "themselves out"
"His lips shot open" "with a loud smack—" "we almost" "laughed aloud but"
"he spoke with a" "rich deep voice:" "'The radiance" "of a death"
"cannot now" "justify the" "travail," "the travail of" "this" "hard life . . ."

"The tyrant robs us" "of transcendence" "by making it" "all we can have . . ."
"our ordinary" "coinage . . ." "coinage . . ." "Who wants it?" "Can we
not have something small," "a bit of daily" "air to breathe?'" "The man
went silent" "The red lights" "around the victim" "went out" "Everyone

turned away" "& filed silently" "into connecting cars" "We followed,"
"we followed"

" 'All inspiration" "comes from here,'" "the tyrant whispered" "as we changed cars" " 'All stories," "all drama," "all poetry" "come from here now" "My heart" "is theirs" "I feel all" "I feel as they feel" "What else can" "a heart be like," "tell me that?'" " 'Your heart"

"is not your own," "is composed of" "the hearts of others," "lives of others" "Blue stone" "is your true heart," "your only true heart'" " 'They cannot exist" "without me" "Was the woman" "crying blood" "not crying my blood?'" " 'She should not be weeping blood" "She should be

crying" "free water," "free water," "transparent water" "We must see the world" "through our tears" "Not weep" "the thick substance" "of another's" "reality," "another's" "reality . . .' "

" 'Let's get off at" "River Street,' " "the tyrant said" "We
soon arrived there," "exited" " 'Have you ever" "seen the river"
"the stop is named for?' he asked" "I shook my head" " 'Behind the
wall" "Behind this wall,' he said" "He opened" "a ramshackle" "door"

"of boards collapsing," "in a dirty" "bare wall—" "line of black dirt"
"where wall met floor—" "& we were then in" "a damp darkness"
"that smelled of" "something else," "something else than" "only water"
"The tyrant pulled" "a long flashlight" "from the inside" "of his jacket"

"& shone it on" "a river" "running between two" "subway platforms"
"which were quite" "wide apart," "wide apart as" "riverbanks"
"The water—" "but the water" "was red," "red-black" " 'Your blood?' "
"I whispered" " 'Yes,' " "he said" "The current" "of this river" "was

slow," "quite slow" "Into" "the lit area—" "of bloody liquid"
"lit by the flashlight—" "flowed something" "on the surface," "a dark
cloth, a" "black tatter," "a small" "black-handkerchief-like" "fragment
with tattered edge" " 'It is mine" "It is something" "of mine,' I

said to him," " 'How can I get it?' " "Alarmed," "alarmed-seeming,"
"he snapped the" "flashlight off" "I had sensation then" "of enlargement of,"
"enlargement of" "my eyes" "And could see" "the black cloth" "Could
see it" "in the dark" "Time slowed" "as it had" "at the entrance"

"to the subway" "when I had had to" "cross over" "the abandoned track"
"full of rats—" "But I was conscious" "in this dream, this" "dream-like"
"real happening" "For I was winged" "Slow & fast," "wide-winged
quiet-winged," "I hovered" "next instant," "mid-instant" "above the

black thing" "Then plucked it up" "in my beak—" "which felt like having"
"stiff-fingered teeth—" "I was soon back" "on the platform," "stood"
"as a woman," "holding" "the black fabric" "in my hand" "The tyrant
now switched" "the flashlight back on"

"I held the cloth up" "before the beam of" "the flashlight"
"It was diaphanous," "black-airy" "'May I see it . . .'" "the tyrant said"
"& began stretching" "his hand towards it" "I popped it into" "my mouth,"
"into my mouth &" "swallowed it" "Swallowed" "it down" "There was

within me" "at once" "a bleak dawning," "a sky turning" "from ob-
sidian" "to sickly" "bluish light" "'Why was my memory," "my memory,"
"floating in your" "heartsblood?' I cried" "'I must have" "let go of it"
"It was too painful" "I loosed it from me" "& gave it back to you"

"back to your body," "from where its pain came" "My name is" "Alette"
"My brother" "died in battle'" "I sank" "to the ground &" "sat,"
"sat & thought of him—" "his pure profile," "his head's shape" "un-
changed since babyhood—" "well modeled," "rounded well-made above

delicate" "neck's nape" "neck's nape" "The tyrant stood stiffly near"
"holding out" "the flashlight" "with an almost military" "cast to"
"his demeanor" "He was again" "deeply moved" "& thus I found" "my anger,"
"my life-" "giving anger" "'He died,' I began again," "'when you last

fought . . ." "yourself" "When two of your . . ." "warrior masks," "two of
your leaders" "last fought," "when two armies" "were amassed from"
"the subway populace'" "'Men fight,' he said" "'Men fight" "Don't you
think they must sometimes?" "And there's a shape to—" "an intensity"

"to battle—" "to war—" "a proximity to life & death—" "that captures
many men's" "imaginations . . .'" "'That's exactly what women" "are en-
slaved to,'
I said dully" "'But this is all a cliché" "All a cliché, anyway"
"I don't" "want to live" "in a cliché,' I said" "'Your" "house of insults"

"of science," "of art," "your trivial politics," "your inspiration"
"drawn from the hardships" "of others . . ." "my grief for" "my brother"
"so moving" "to you . . ." "I must" "have been searching" "for him"
"as well" "Or I was searching" "for her voice—" "the headless"

"woman's voice—" "so that I could" "speak to you'" "'Beautiful,'"
"he murmured" "'It is not *beautiful*" "It is what was!'" "I was nearly"
"screaming now" "'He is in" "the black lake" "I have been there too"
"It is all" "that there is" "that isn't you," "that isn't you"

"Infinity" "isn't you!'" "'But it's all" "so beautiful," "so moving,'"
"he kept murmuring" "with tears" "in his eyes"

“ ‘You are vulnerable” “somewhere near here,’ ” “I said to him”
“ ‘If there is blood,” “all this blood,” “if in this river” “flows your blood,”
“there must be flesh” “somewhere . . . ’ ” “ ‘It has long since” “turned to
concrete,” “to brick & steel,’ he said” “ ‘*I am not vulnerable*”

“*anywhere*’ ” “His eyes” “tore into mine, but” “there was a glint there,”
“I thought,” “of hesi-tancy” “ ‘I will find” “that place,’ I said &”
“became an” “owl again” “contracting lengthwise,” “spreading widthwise,”
“becoming” “wings & eyes—” “such a lightness—” “I felt hardly formed”

“I began to fly” “along the” “bloody river,” “corridored river,”
“looking into” “the darkness” “for any trace of” “fleshy softness,”
“fleshy softness”

"The tyrant" "pursued me, running," "at first" "as I flew" "I began slowly," "searching, looking" "Stopped & hovered sometimes" "He lunged at me" "once or twice" "as I flew low" "But I was quickness," "speed of thought," "unhinderable reflex" "As I became" "used to my search"

"& speeded up, he" "fell behind" "Then he disappeared" "entirely"
"I had no mind now" "but flew & looked" "My brother's image" "had vanished"
"Had vanished" "from my thoughts" "Beneath a lightbulb" "I saw myself"
"on the surface" "of the river:" "unnuanced owl eyes" "amid feathers"

"distorted, shadowy" "in liquid thickness" "Along the river, here & there,"
"people slept" "huddled upright" "or spread out" "on the concrete"
"I saw" "a strangely shaped," "almost potato-" "shaped man," "bald,"
"thick-necked—" "his head was like" "a rounded neck—" "pale, coarsely

fleshed," "peeled-looking," "his facial features" "sketchy-seeming"
"He stood chanting" "to himself," "'Am I" "the man the father?" "Am I"
"the man the father?'" "And someone else" "in bandages," "someone wound with" "strips of white gauze—" "like a mummy—" "wandered up & down,"

"up & down this" "heart river—" "a man," "a tall man," "who would scream or weep" "or cry out" "these words or" "a variant:" "'Where is"
"my body," "my sacred" "body?" "Where is my corpus" "sagrada? . . .'"
"Cardboard," "bottles, faeces," "unnamed dirt blacknesses" "were strewn"

"upon the platform—" "the river" "itself" "was plain," "unlittered,"
"glittered redly," "red, black & silver" "beneath the" "occasional lightbulb"

"Thus I followed" "the river" "as it curved," "curved & straightened,"
"unhindered," "unpartitioned" "Finally" "I heard a motor—"
"the tyrant" "was now driving" "a small" "open vehicle" "Had caught
up with me" "in this cart" "He rode beneath me" "a short distance;"

"then I saw that," "ahead of us," "the river branched into" "several
small streams" "But their paths thence" "were cloaked in blackness:"
"all" "illumination" "ceased where" "these rivulets began" "I paused"
"& hovered" "at the edge of" "the darkness" "The tyrant stopped too"

"& shouted up at me," "'You act wrongly," "act wrongly" "The order"
"of things" "has" "its own wisdom" "formed by everyone's" "will'"
"I opened" "my mouth" "to reply, but" "my mouth" "was a beak"
"The hoo hoo hoo hoo" "that issued from me" "echoed" "off the walls,"

"filled the corridor," "filled my owl self" "I faced him downwards,"
"circled looking down" "Loosed a slow stream" "of owl sound,"
"a stream of crying" "mournful notes," "mixed with screams &" "low
growls," "with scornful" "laughing sounds" "His eyes were frozen wide,"

"his face tense," "bone-naked," "pure in crisis" "He stared &"
"stared at me" "Searched me out, but" "I wasn't there" "I wasn't"
"there at all" "I continued" "to sound at him" "in purity," "in purity,"
"in purity" "of owl's own" "Then I flew into" "the dark"

"The pupils" "of my owl eyes" "grew even larger" "I could see,
faintly outlined," "the rivulets" "& their nearby" "destinations"
"Beyond the threshold" "of the darkness" "the river's corridor"
"widened" "into an immense chamber" "The streams flowed there into"

"a semicircle" "of grottos," "room-sized" "smooth cupolaed caves—"
"each stream had" "its own grotto" "There were five of each"
"Four of the grottos" "were constructed" "of gray cement," "made by
techno-" "logical process" "But one grotto" "was pink" "soft &

undulant," "uneven," "soft & fleshy," "soft & fleshy—" "though
firm too," "rather palate-like" "It was surrounded by" "a high"
"spiked mesh fence" "with a padlocked door" "A sign hung" "on the
door:" "*This fence is*" "*electrified*" "I easily" "flew over it"

"I flew" "beneath the round" "flesh roof" "of the grotto"
"There was a light switch on the wall" "which I pushed up" "with my beak" "A pearl-" "like fixture" "now illuminated" "the cave"
"The bloody rivulet" "flowed" "into a small well" "in the floor,"

"sunk beneath" "the flesh floor" "near the entrance" "to the grotto"
"But also in the floor—" "in its center—" "something grew,"
"a small plant" "that was rooted" "in that flesh," "a bush of"
"different textures," "though symmetrical" "in form:" "It was

composed of" "long-fingered" "stiff branches" "But it was leafless"
"& each branch had" "a different surface" "One branch was furry"
"with brown" "short thick bear's fur" "One branch" "was a length"
"of reptilian skin," "thin & dry" "like a shed snakeskin," "though

stiff" "& erect here:" "it was palely" "brown-striped" "One branch"
"was vegetative—" "but spiky," "dull green" "And one branch"
"was feathered" "with pale small downy feathers" "But one branch seemed to be" "a very thin long human arm" "less than" "two inches

wide—" "a hand small" "as a baby's," "which held" "a dead rose,"
"a dried black dead rose"

"The tyrant" "was near the fence now," "working" "the switch"
"which de-" "electrified it" "Then he unlocked the door" "& entered"
"I panicked" "for the grotto" "was not" "very high" "I flew at its
rear wall" "& extended" "my talon—" "Sliced into" "the flesh wall,"

"clawed it repeatedly" "It began to ooze" "drops of blood, but"
"the wall" "was not vital" "to the tyrant" "I heard him laugh,"
"laugh behind me" "I turned & faced him" "A white liquid" "now seeped"
"through the arm" "of his jacket" "'You can't kill me!'" "he shouted,"

"exultantly," "then rushed at me" "I flew out" "of the grotto"
"He sat down" "& laughed again," "then reclined next to the bush"
"'Come & keep me" "company" "Keep me company!' he called" "'We're both
weary now" "Let's rest awhile" "together'" "I could in fact"

"barely fly" "'Why not?' I thought—" "& was beside him" "a woman,"
"a tired woman" "'Even if,' he said," "'you pierced through," "all the
way through" "these walls with" "your talon," 'I would not die:"
"it is such" "a small part of me," "this grotto . . ." "Flesh is not my"

"nature now . . .'" "But I thought that" "the wound" "I had made in"
"his arm" "was tiring him," "as well as" "the physical" "exertion"
"But what use was" "his fatigue to me," "if he was" "immortal?"
"'What is this bush?'" "I asked him" "But he had fallen" "asleep"

"I sat & stared at" "the bush" "Gradually" "I discovered" "that the
attenuated" "armlike branch" "was making small" "twisting movements,"
"slight motions" "periodically" "And the flower," "the dead rose that"
"it held," "began to change" "Its petals" "became moist & full,"

"became dewy red . . . " "The tyrant muttered" "in his sleep" "Then his
face" "composed itself," "became youthful-looking, tranquil"
"The whole bush now came alive" "The branches rustled" "& touched
each other:" "The scaled branch lost" "its dryness," "its thinness

of molt" "& gleamed sinuously" "Likewise the" "other branches"
"became more vital" "& lustrous" "The green of" "the green branch"
"deepened" "The feathers broadened" "& took on color" "The brown fur"
"grew longer . . . " "I understood" "what to do now" "& searched myself"

"for a cruelty" "& temporary" "heartlessness" "I didn't know of"
"in myself:" "my owl self" "had to do this" "But I thought" "my
woman's body" "had factually" "to do this" "I closed my eyes,"
"saw the winged" "shadow shape of" "my owl" "I seemed to empty" "I

extended" "my arms in front of me" "Grasped the bush" "in my hands"
"& yanked it out of" "the ground" "Pulled it up by" "the roots"
"which were long threadlike red," "glistening" "with blood" "But
one root," "one slender strand," "would not dislodge" "from the ground"

"I pulled as hard as" "I could—" "heard the tyrant" "stir & moan,"
"make, still in his sleep," "low pained moans" "I dropped" "the bush
suddenly" "Rose, rushed up" "in weightless smallness" "Hovered wide-
winged," "an owl again" "Then settled on the floor" "& with my talon"

"dug into it," "the fleshy floor" "I gouged out the" "stubborn
last root" "Blood spurted up" "in a small jet" "Then I changed back"
"into a woman," "sat breathless" "& blood-spattered" "near the
tyrant" "still tossing, moaning," "not yet" "fully conscious"

"There was" "a full moment" "of silence" "& stillness"
"which spread out" "around my action" "I felt encircled by" "time-
lessness" "As if in" "another realm" "I had not acted," "had never
acted" "Then the tyrant jerked awake," "convulsed & clutched at"

"his chest" "Eyes enormous," "amazed" "He spoke with difficulty,"
"in fits:" "'I think . . . " "you have killed me . . . " "I am . . . " "really
dying' " "He seemed so" "bewildered" " 'How could you be" "this cruel?"
"And do you not" "kill yourself?" "your own culture . . . " "soul's breath?' "

" 'I'm killing no one" "You are not real" "You said so" "yourself,' I
said" " 'Forms in dreams . . . " "forms in dreams . . . ' " "I searched within"
"for right words" " 'I will change the" "forms in dreams' " "I lifted"
"the dead plant" "& flung it" "across the grotto" " 'Starting"

"from dreams," "from dreams we" "can change," "will change" "In
dreams," "in dreams, now," "you will die" "You will die' "
"He turned" "away from me" "Lay looking upward," "wide-eyed, panting"
"His body seemed" "to become" "more & more" "transparent," "lose

substance" "From within it," "within him," "a ghostly tableau
emerged," "hovered," "above his body," "was performed in" "air above him:"
"There was a thicket" "in which a knight" "lay dying" "on the ground"
"A woman tended him," "bent over him" "in ancient" "Greek costume"

"But she" "was a skeleton" "with long hair" "She spoke & told him:"
" 'What you have made me—" "what you now see—" "is your consort"
"in eternity . . . ' " "The knight took" "her bone hand" "They clasped
hands," "the scene dissolving"

“ ‘Have you” “no forgiveness?’ ” “the tyrant turned his face” “to me”
“ ‘The question” “has no meaning,” “has no meaning,’ ” “I said”
“ ‘For when you ask” “me that” “I am an owl . . . ’ ”
“ ‘Your wings are covering me,’ ” “he said” “Then he died”

"The red river" "stopped flowing—" "the small streams" "became still" "And the light" "went out" "The light went out," "a door swung open" "Near the grotto," "atop a staircase—" "an iron ladder-" "like staircase—" "a door" "opened out:" "a shaft of" "bright

sunlight" "fell hard against" "the stairs," "against the" "floor below" "But I didn't leave quite yet" "I knelt down" "beside the tyrant" "I supposed" "all lights had gone out," "all doors had opened," "the trains had stopped" "Outside, the veil of" "his thought" "that had

obscured the sky," "would be gone" "I touched his" "so-called body," "then lifted" "his hand:" "it was light as" "a rag" "He had no substance now at all" "So I picked up" "the body" "in my arms—it" "hung down like cloth—" "& proceeded" "to carry him" "up the stairs &"

"outside"

"The city" "looked ancient," "still & ancient" "that morning—"
"all traffic" "had stopped;" "all commerce" "had stopped—"
"bricks were artifacts;" "windows, holes" "in the stillness" "in the
light" "I laid the tyrant down" "on the street," "before the crowd"

"'This is not really" "his body,'" "I said to them," "'The structure
we've just left—" "those around us—" "this city—" "how we've lived,"
"is his body'" "A woman" "then picked him up" "& folded him," "his
clothlike body," "till he was" "a small square shape" "Then she

laid him" "aside" "'Must we continue" "to live in" "this corpse of him?'"
"a man asked" "'We can change it," "of course,'" "someone said,"
"'but the earth, all life here" "is structured on," "conducted through,"
"the medium" "of corpses," "remains of corpses" "Very little"

"that is real" "just vanishes" "when it dies . . .'" "'But can't we make"
"something new now . . .'" "another" "began" "I left them" "& sat down"
"on a curb" "beneath a tree" "to rest & watch awhile," "rest & watch"
"I saw those from" "above the ground" "Their clothes had" "become

unwoven" "They stood half-naked" "here & there," "forms to which"
"thread clung" "like hanks of corn silk" "But they had also"
"lost their voices," "most of their" "vocal powers—" "they whispered"
"to each other" "& retreated" "to the periphery" "of" "the growing

throng" "of those who came from below the ground" "And many" "who
emerged" "into the daylight" "then took shovels," "picks & shovels"
"& began to dig" "holes in the ground" "In places" "the surface"
"of the earth broke" "spontaneously" "Cracked & parted:" "all the

lost creatures" "began to" "emerge" "Come up from" "below the subway"
"From the caves &" "from the dark woods" "I had visited" "they emerged"
"I watched through" "tears of clarity" "many" "forms of being"
"I had never" "seen before" "come to join us" "or come to join us

once more" "Whatever," "whoever," "could be," "was possible," "or
had been" "forgotten" "for long ages" "now joined us," "now
joined us once more" "Came to light" "that morning"

Susan Cataldo, 1992

About the Author

Alice Notley was born in Bisbee, Arizona, on November 8, 1945, and grew up in Needles, California. She was educated at Barnard College and at The Writers Workshop, University of Iowa, receiving the appropriate degrees. During the late sixties and early seventies she lived a peripatetic, rather outlawish poet's life (San Francisco, Bolinas, London, Essex, Chicago) before settling on New York's Lower East Side. For sixteen years there, she was an important force in the eclectic second generation of the so-called New York School of poetry. She has never tried to be anything but a poet, and all her ancillary activities have been directed to that end. She is the author of more than twenty books of poetry, including *At Night the States,* the double volume *Close to Me and Closer . . . (The Language of Heaven)* and *Désamère,* and *How Spring Comes,* which was a winner of the San Francisco Poetry Award. Her *Selected Poems* was published in 1993. She is a two-time NEA grant recipient and the recipient of a General Electric Foundation Award, a NYFA fellowship, and several awards from The Fund for Poetry. She now lives permanently in Paris.